TATTOO

DESIGNS

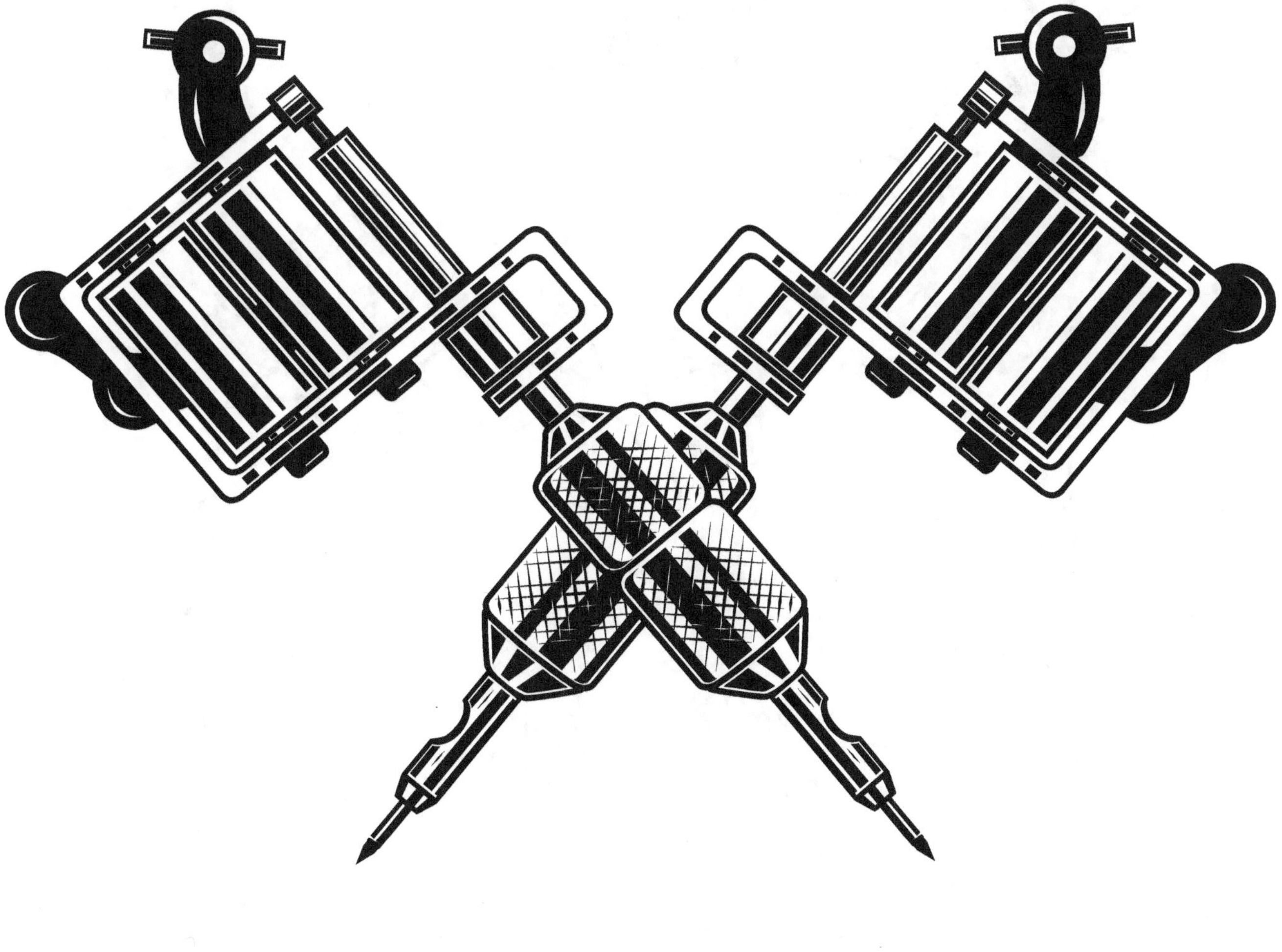

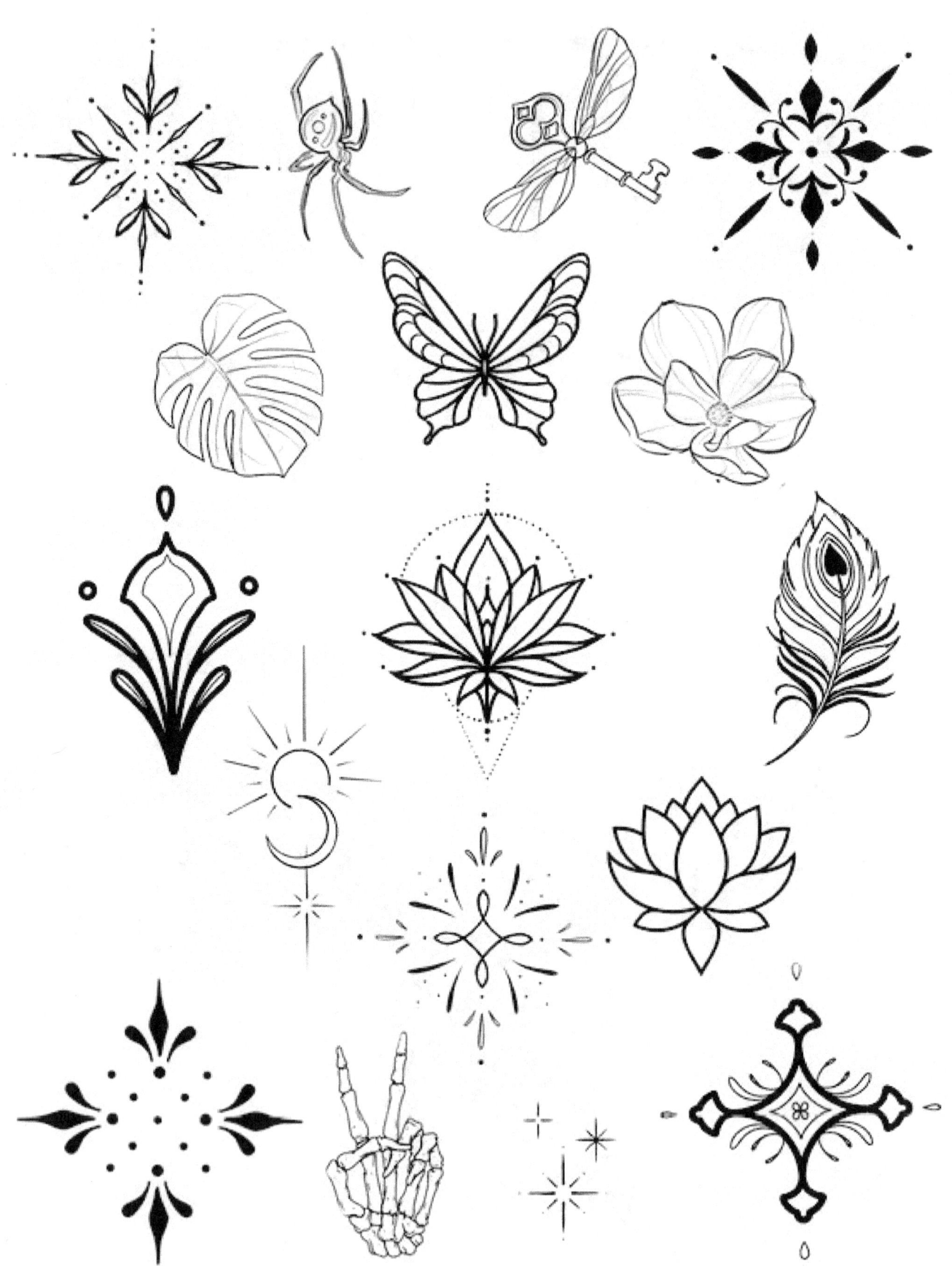

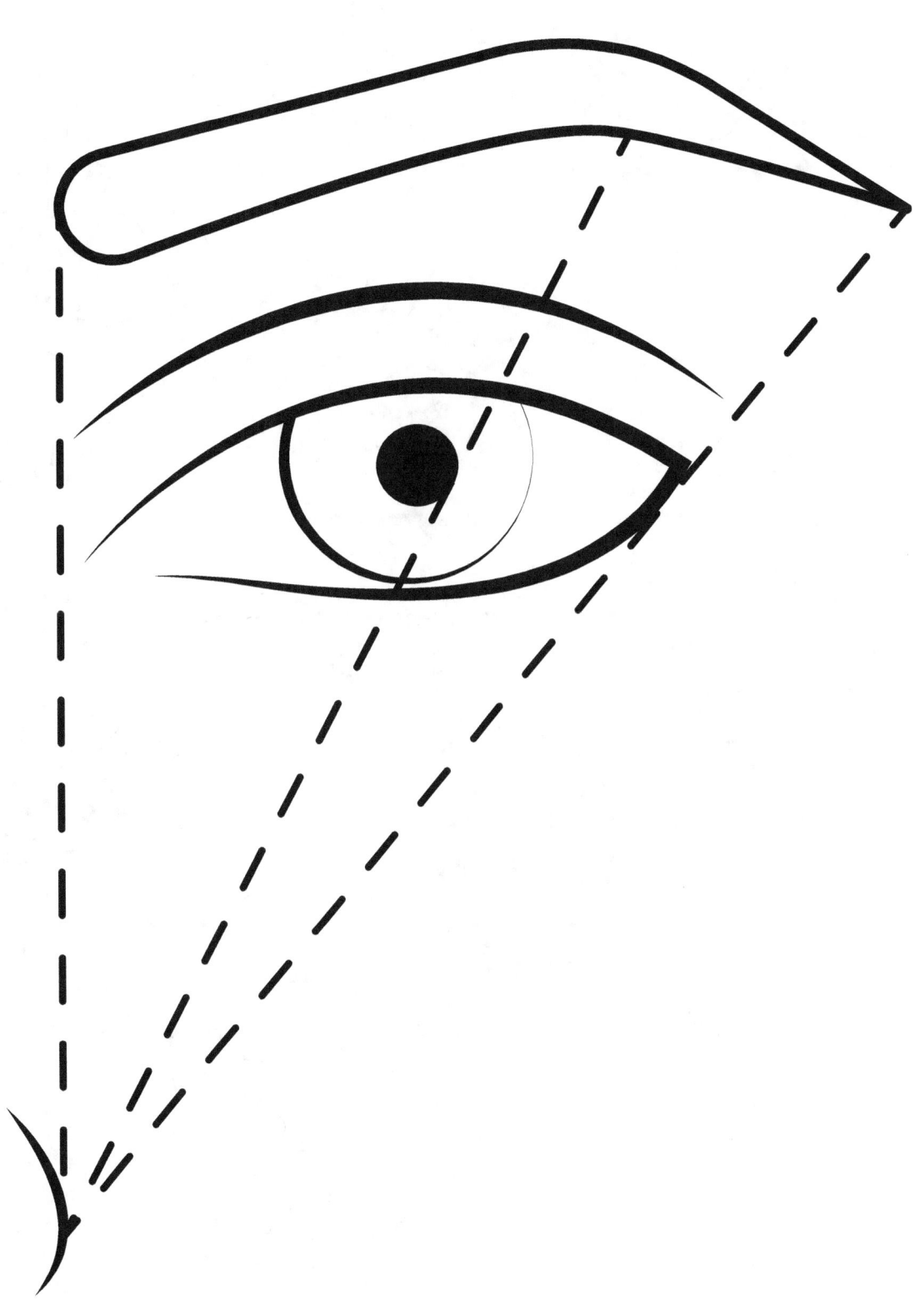

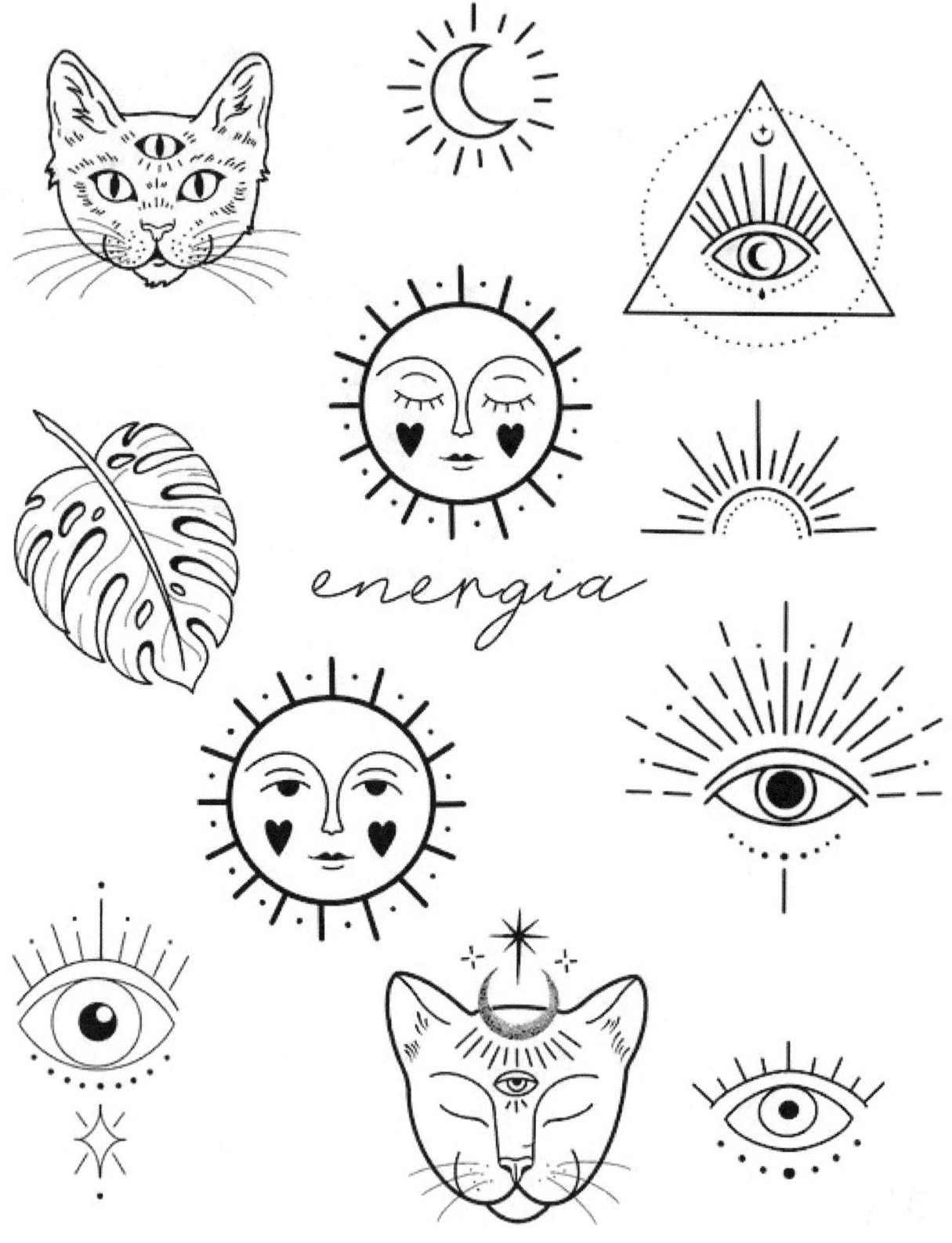

energia

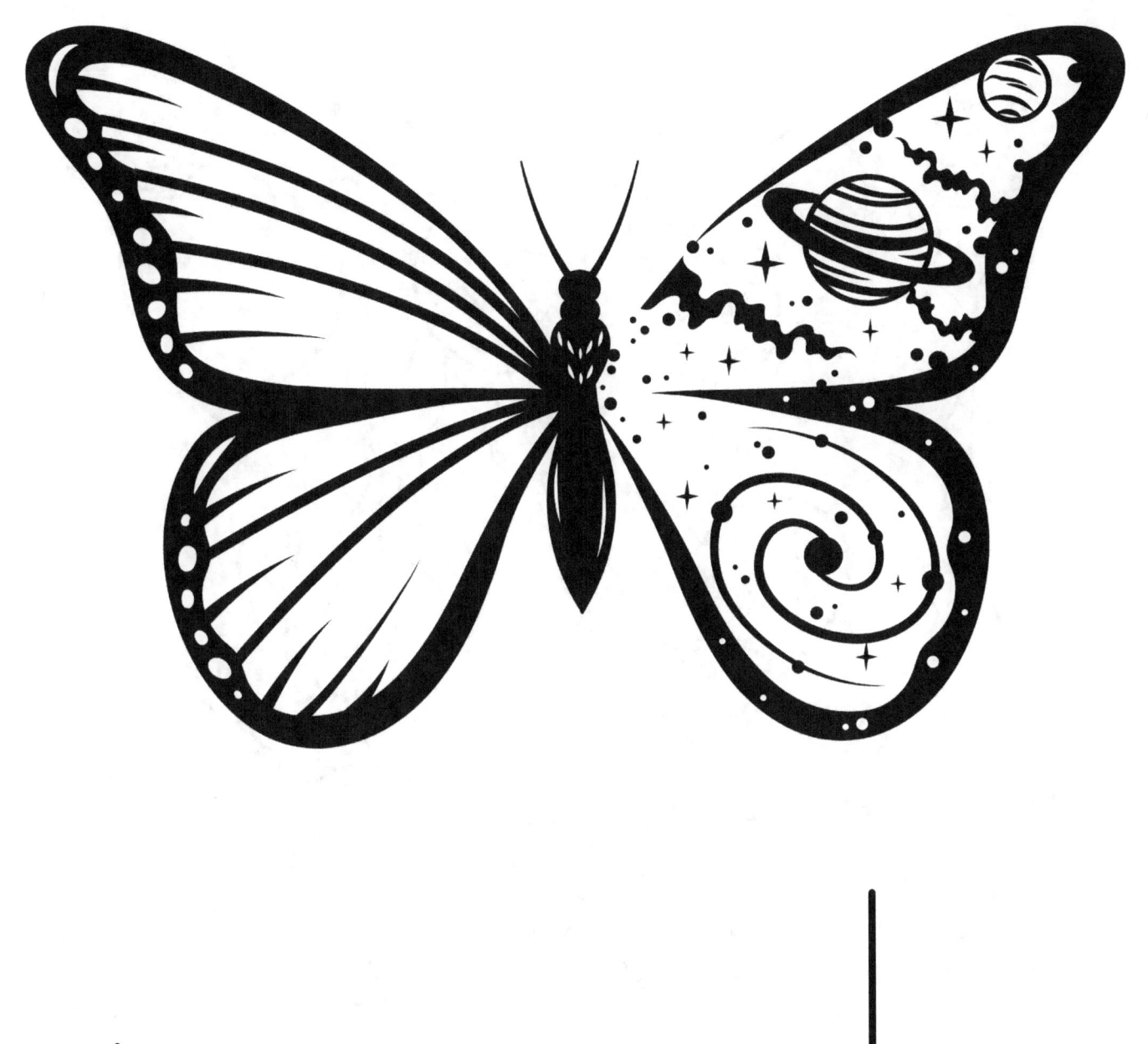

Angel

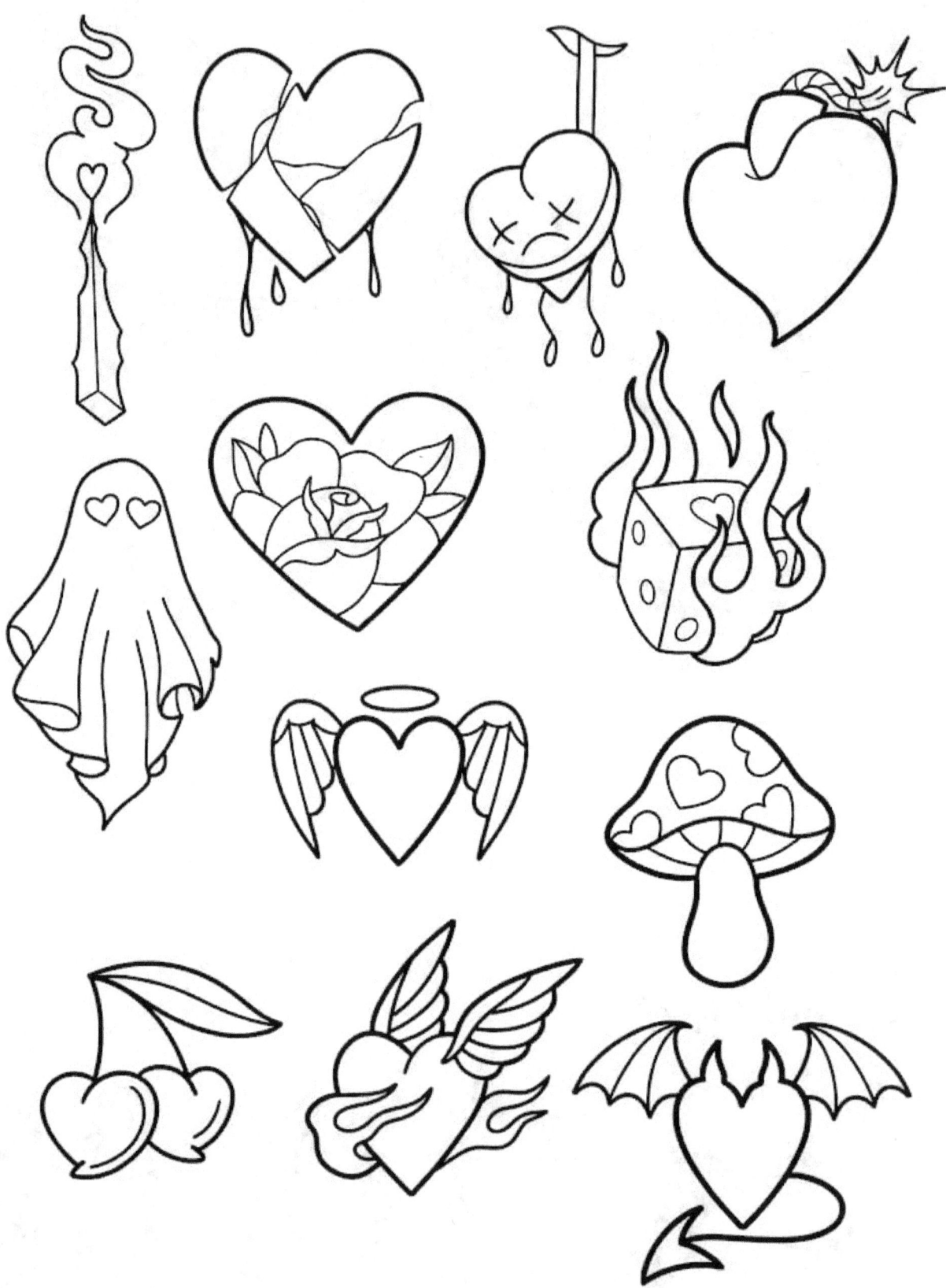

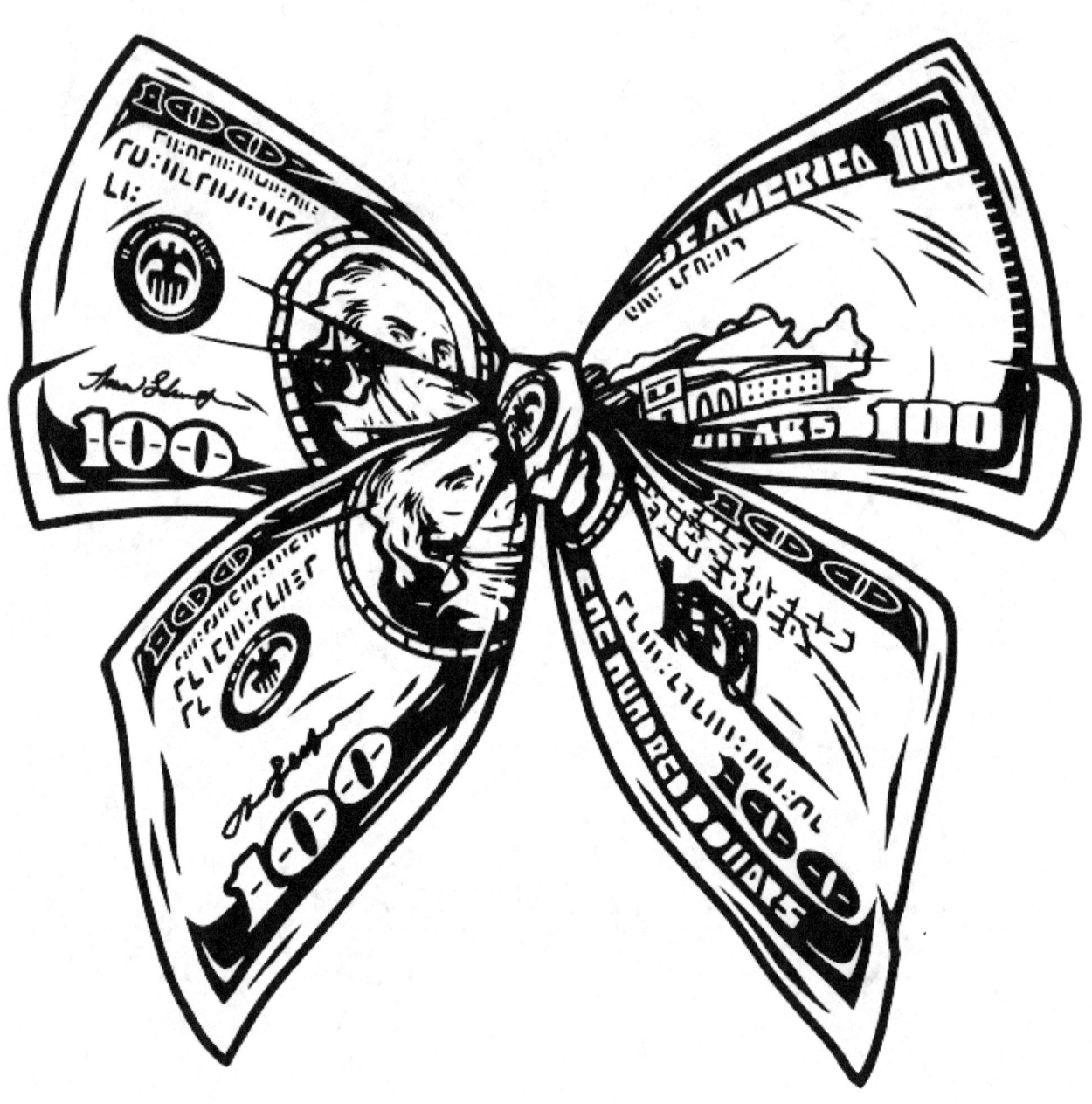

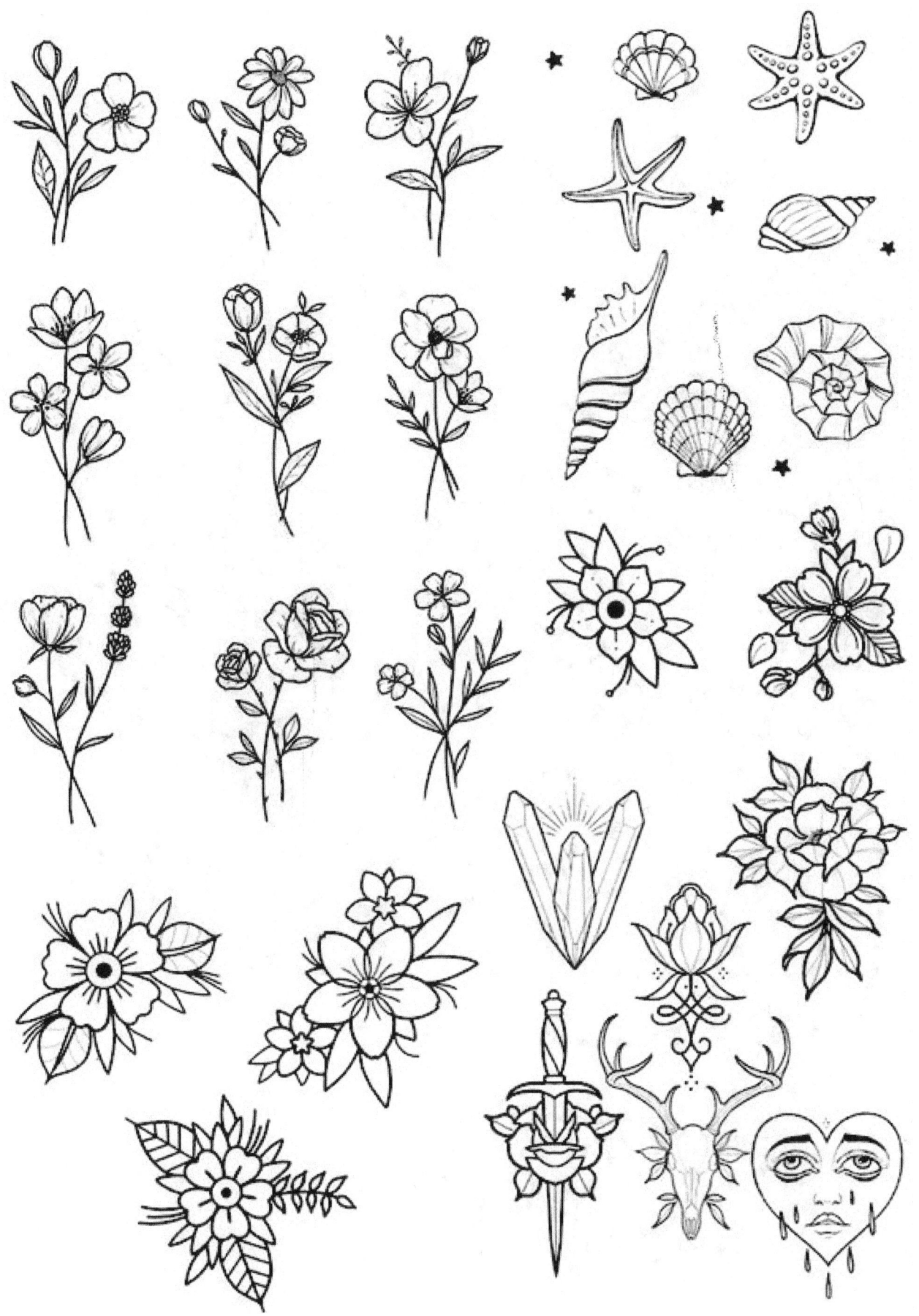

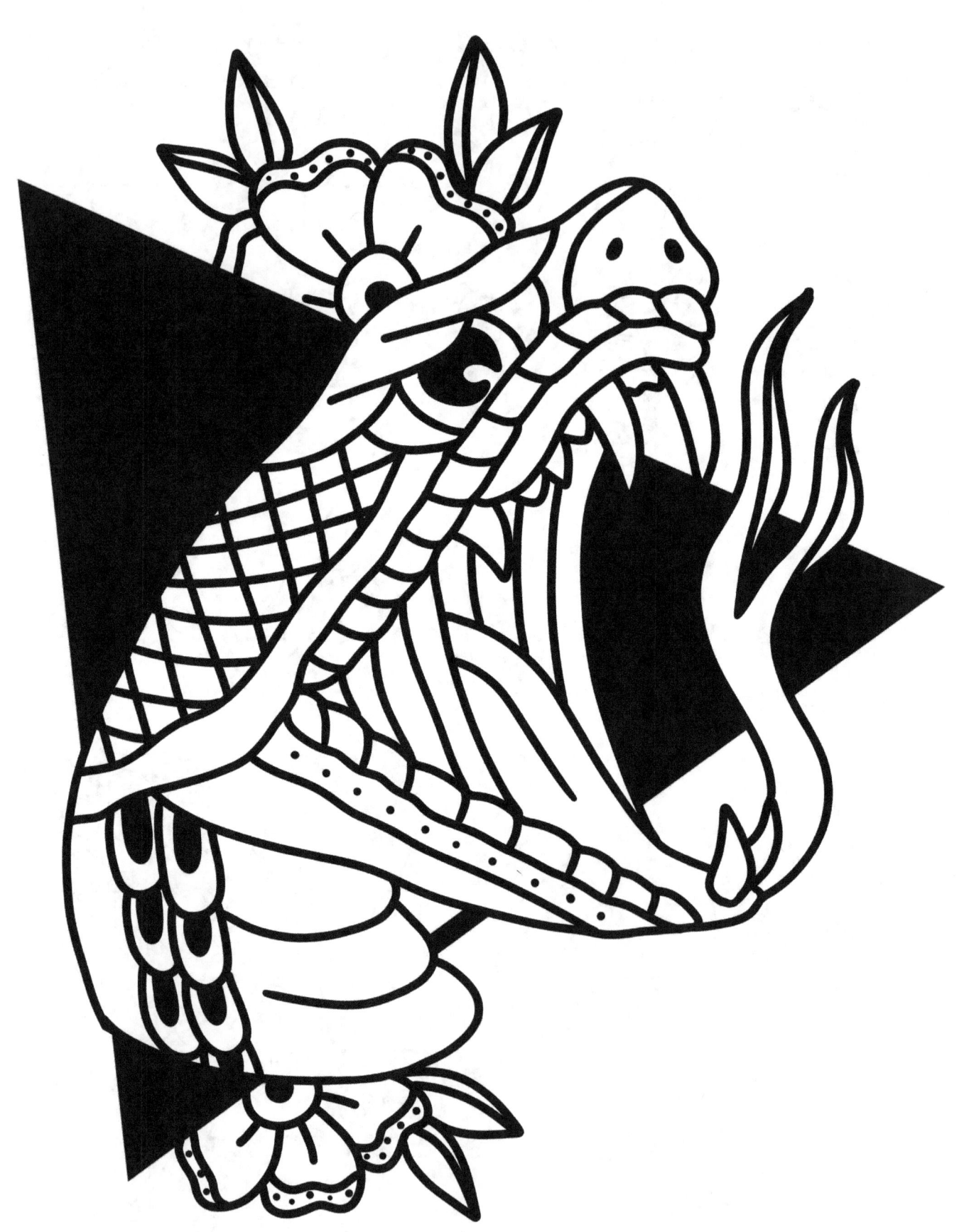

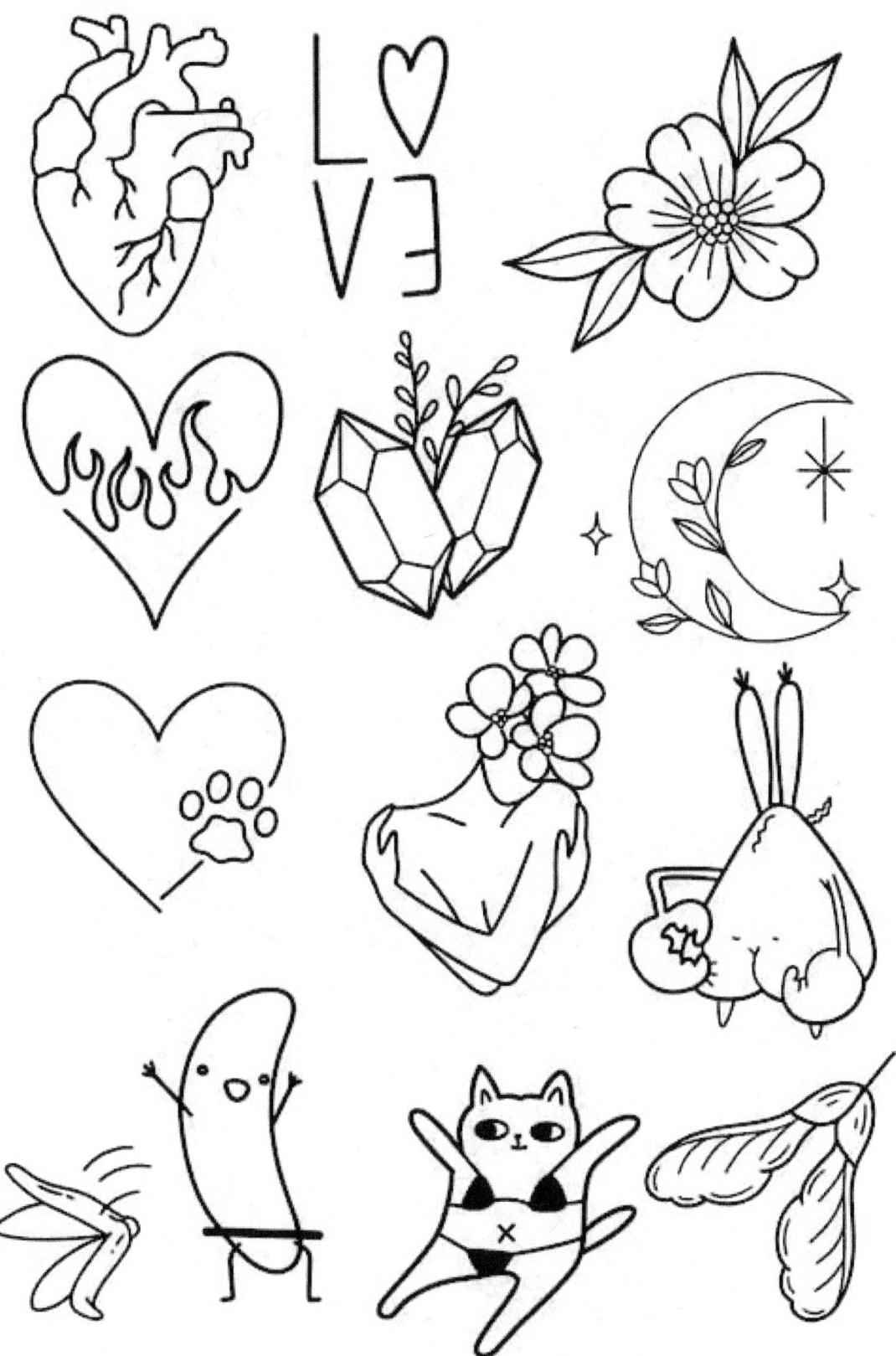

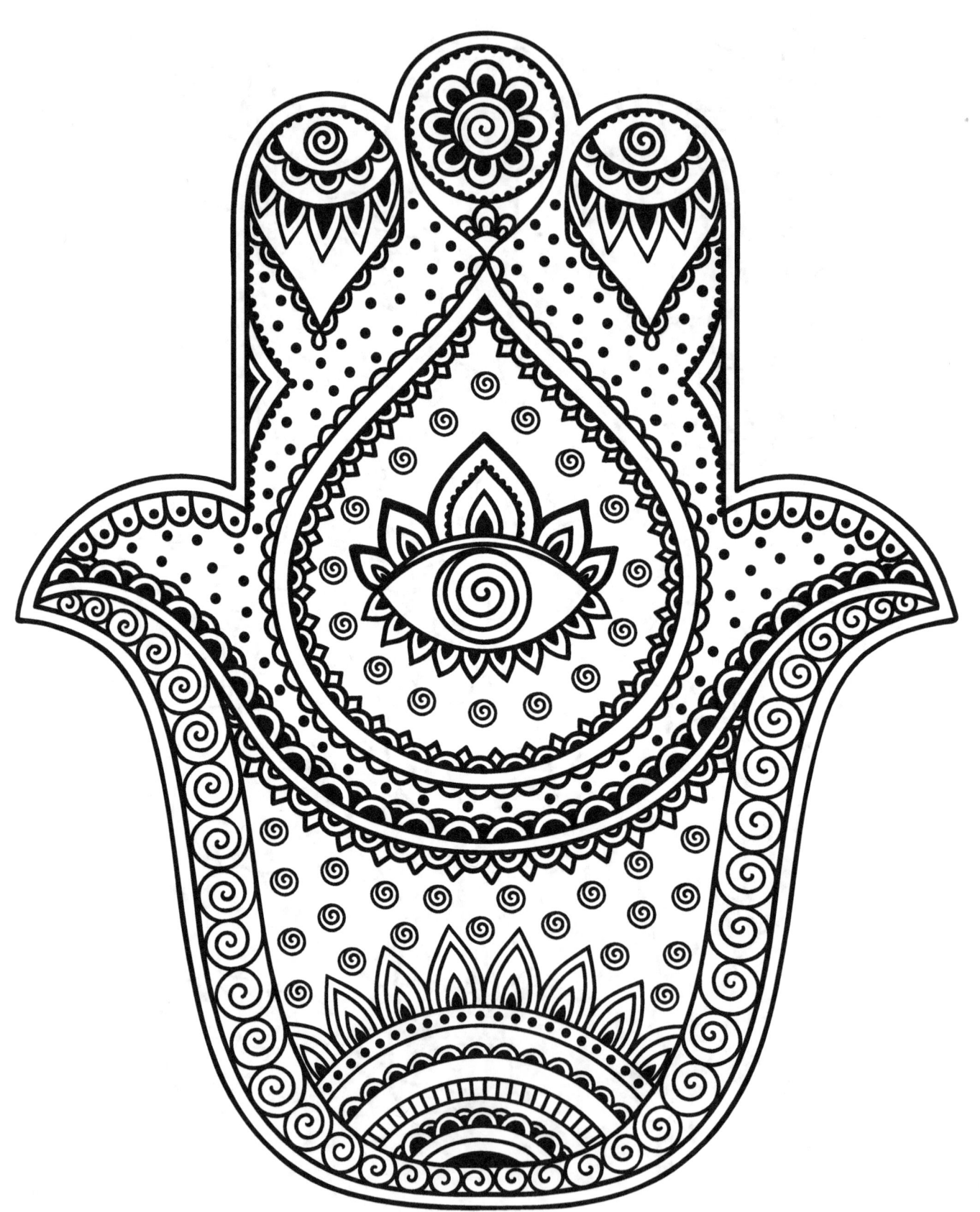

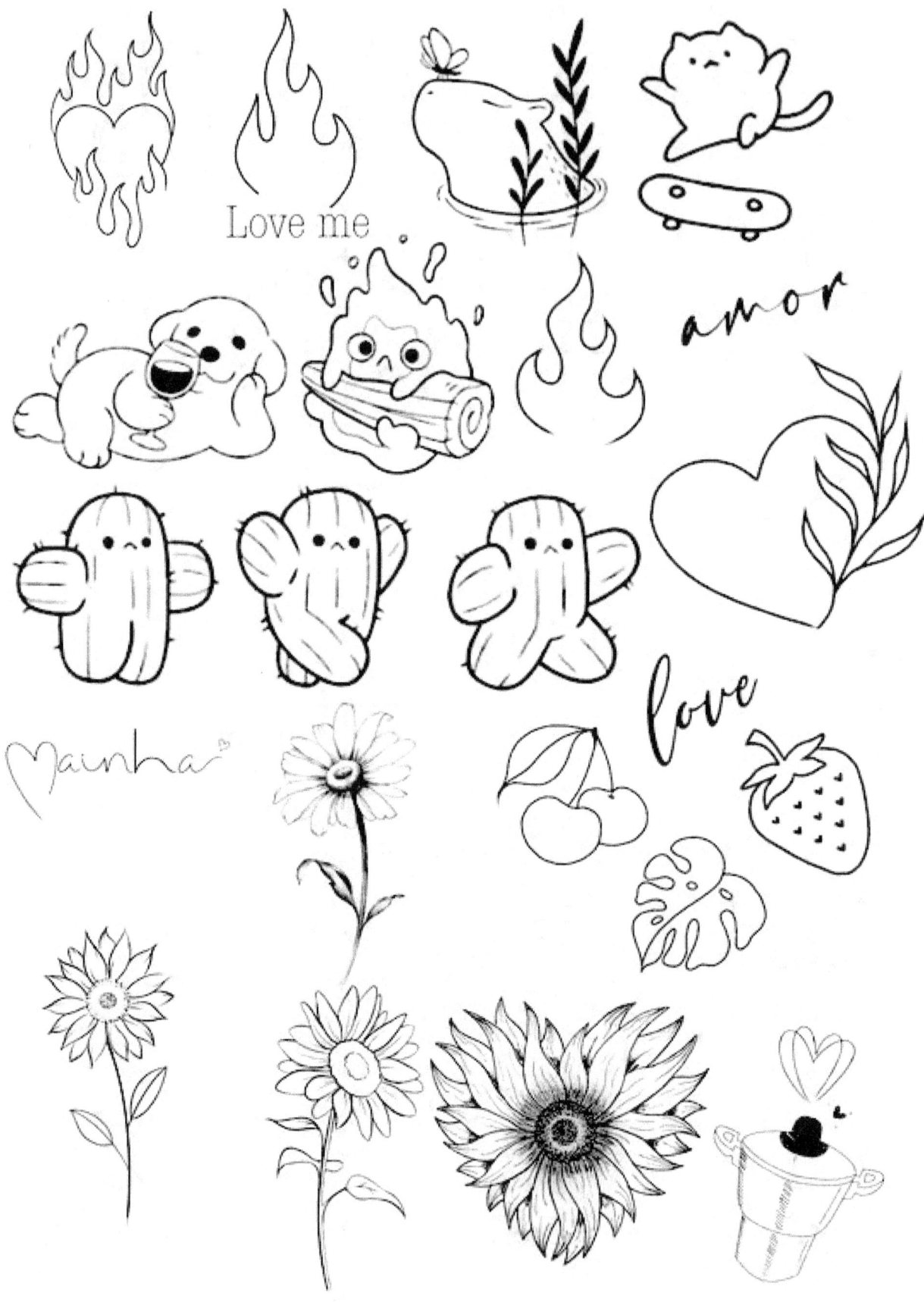

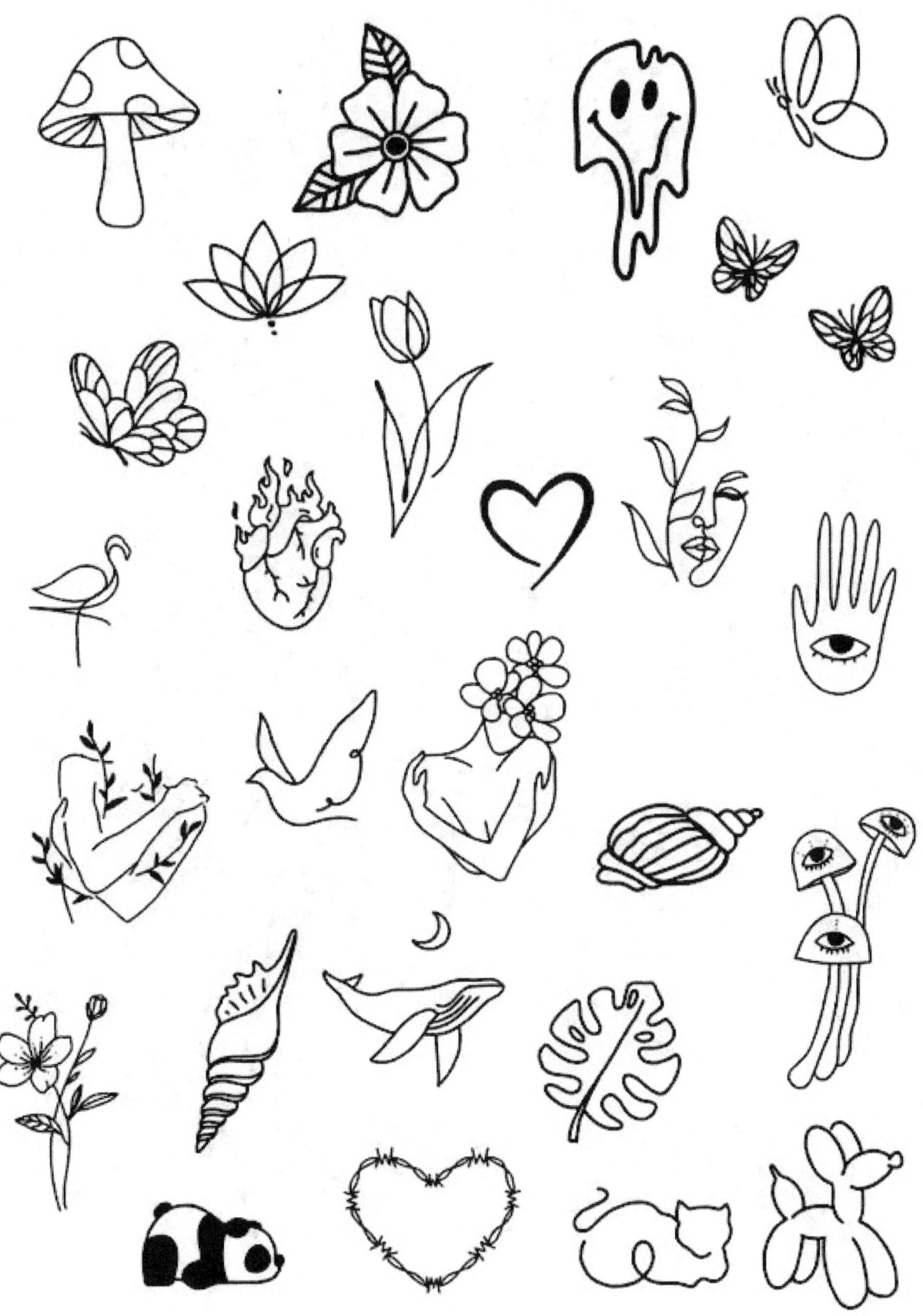

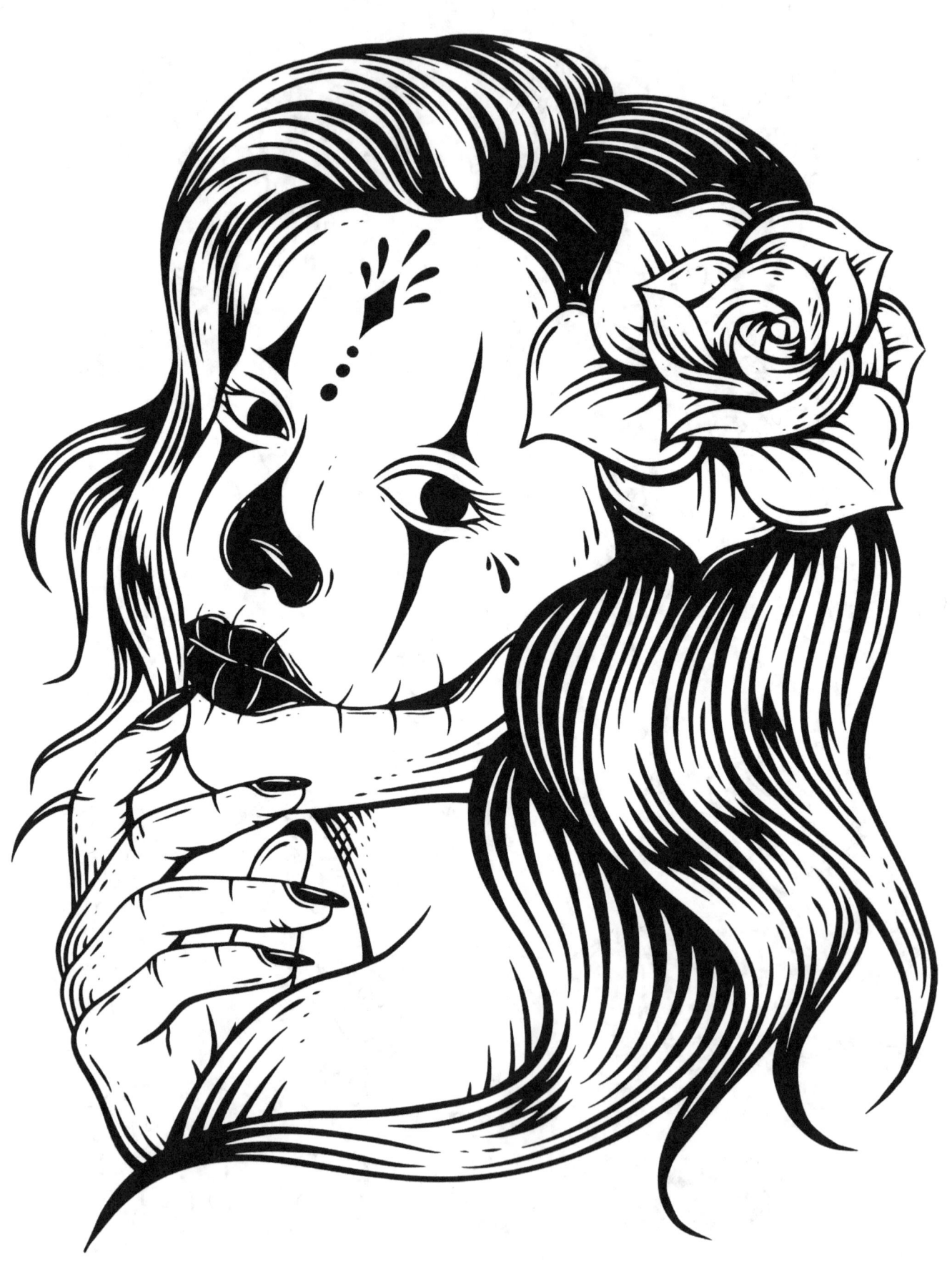

lalala

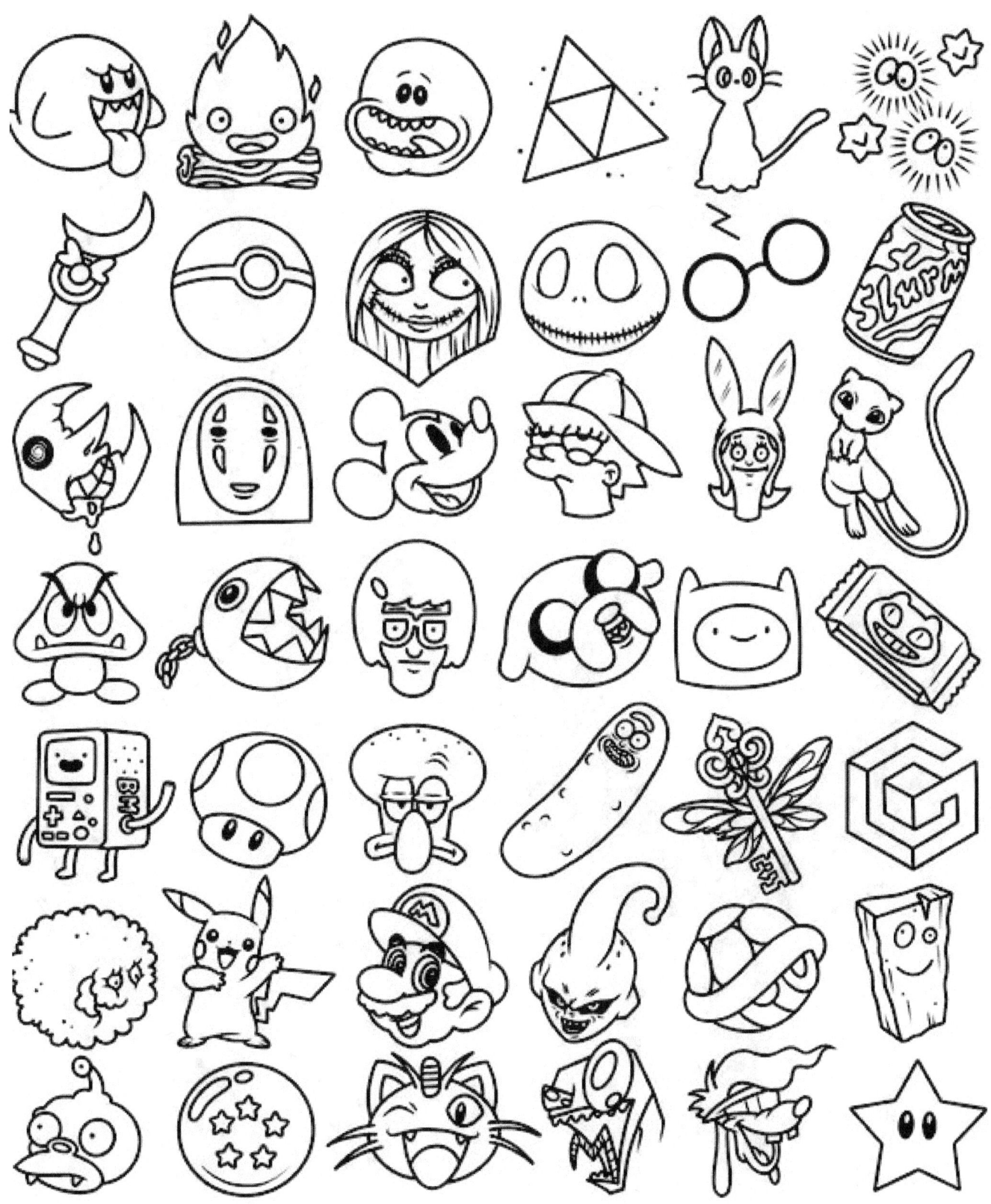

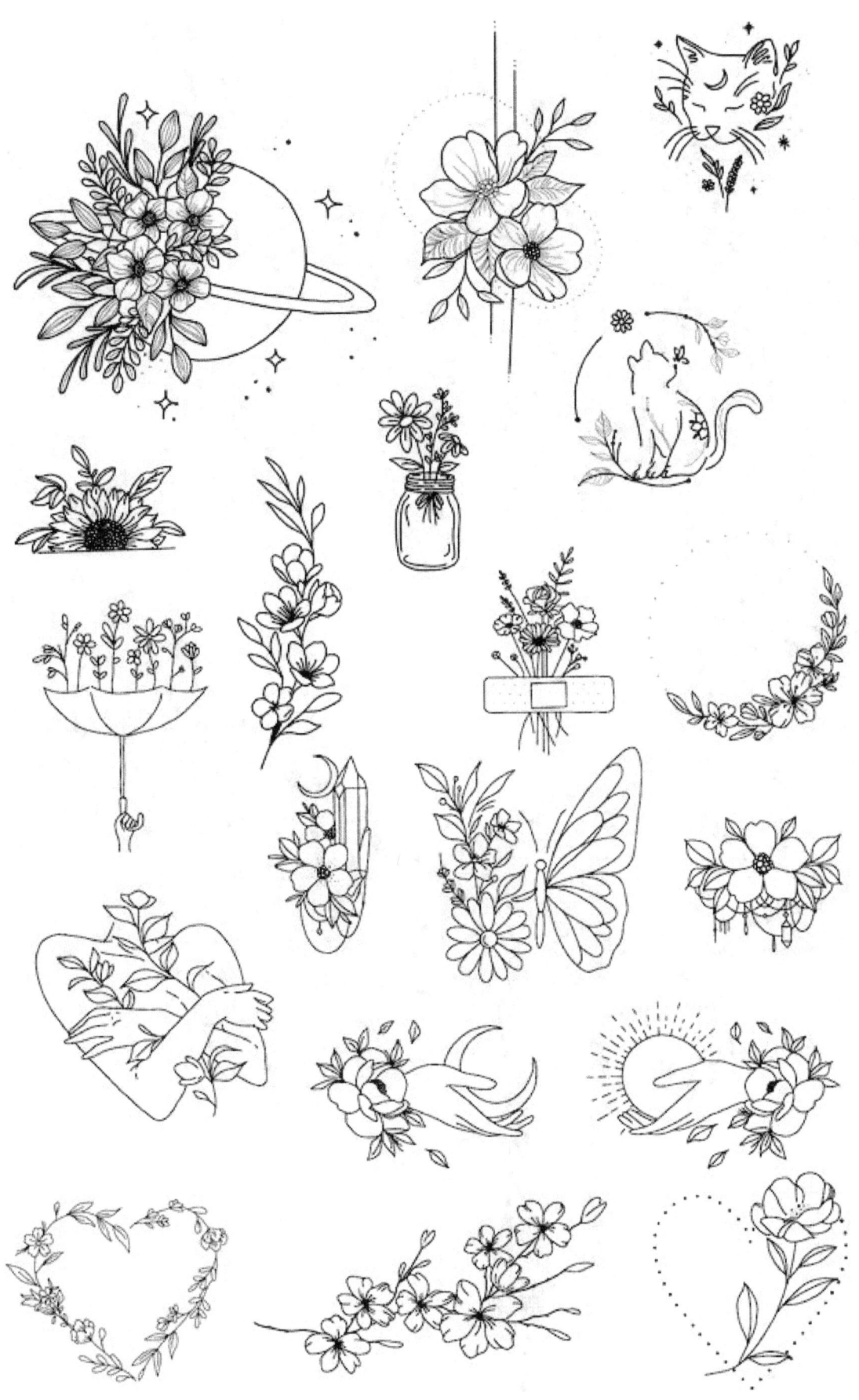

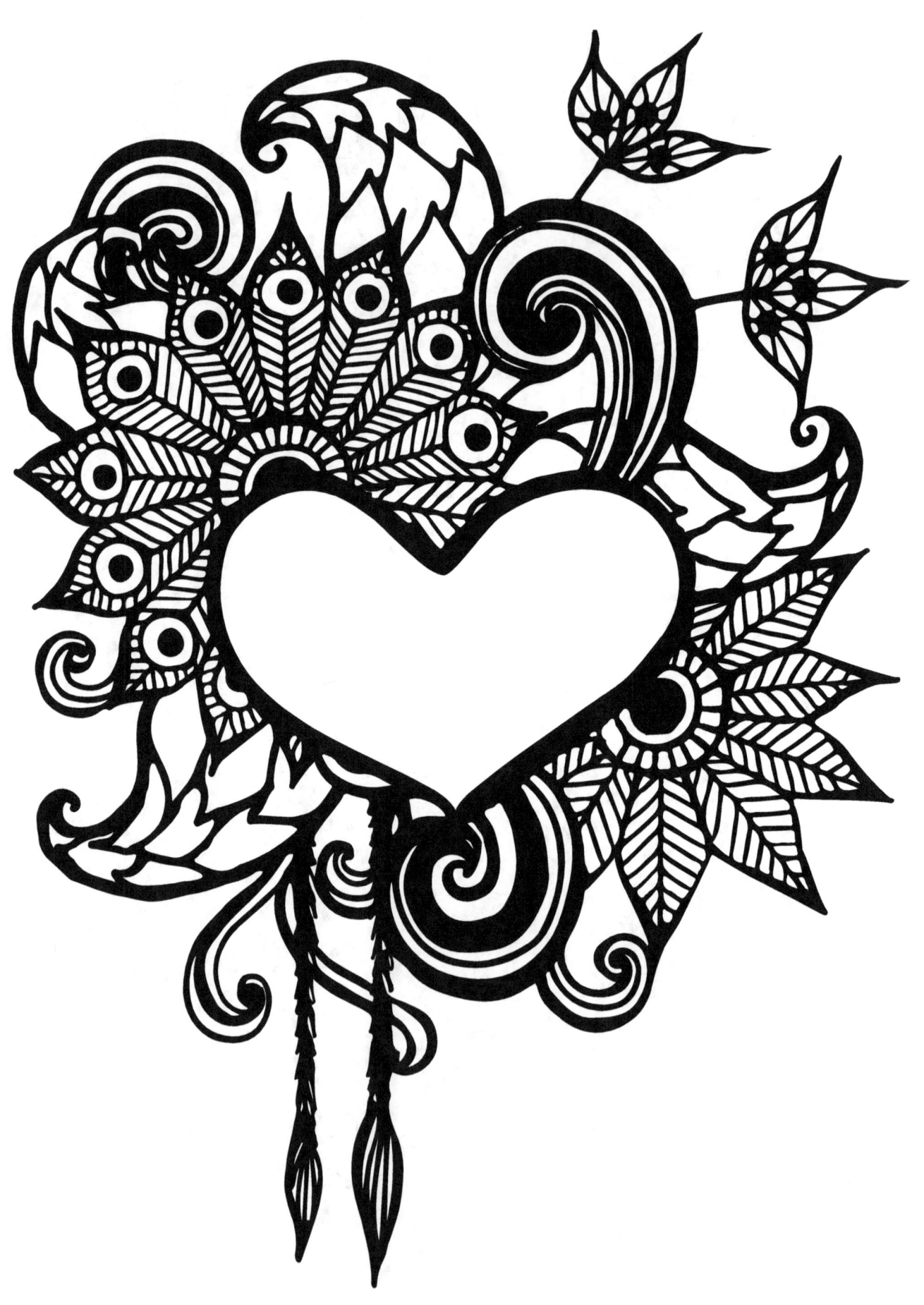

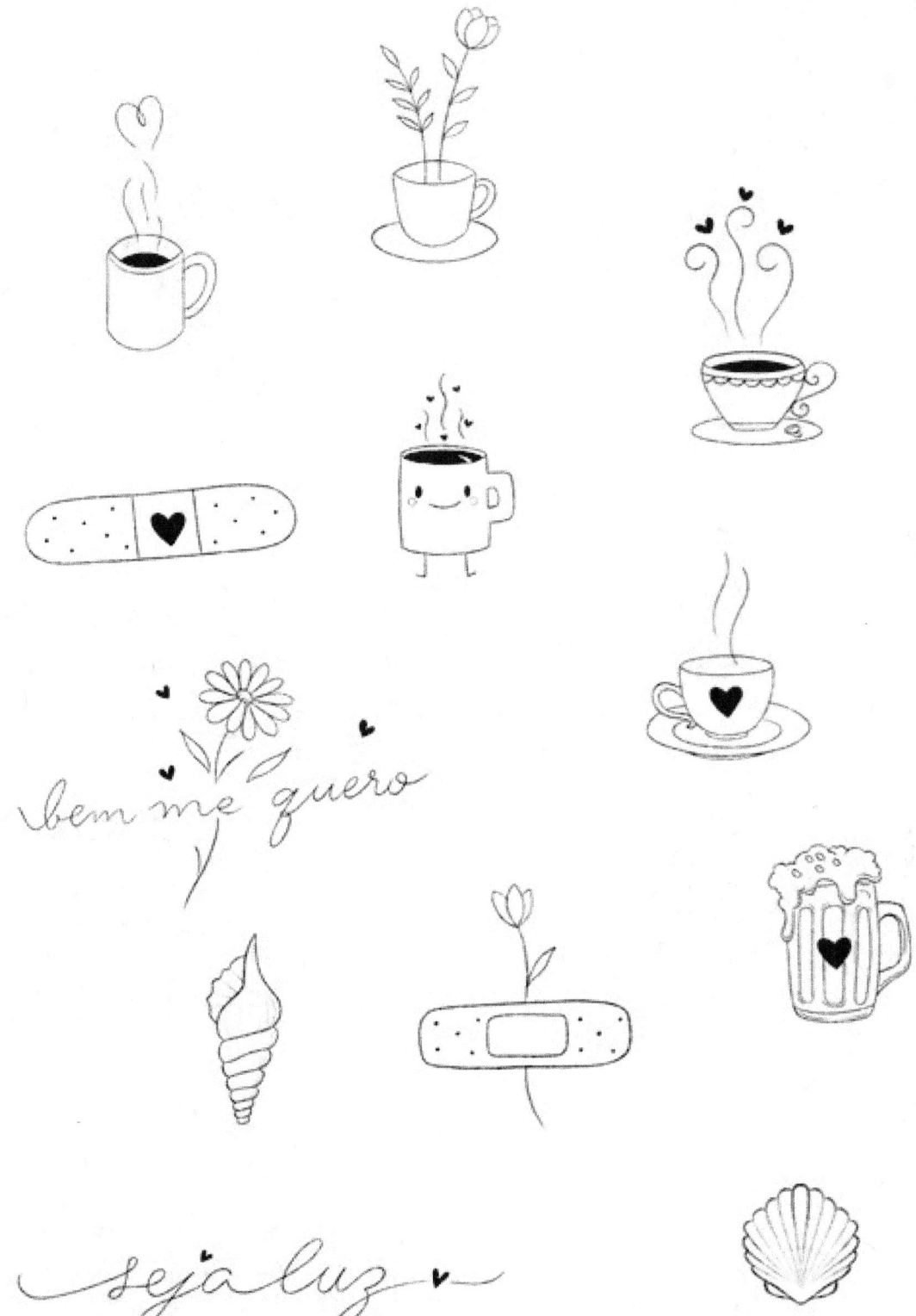

bem me quero

seja luz

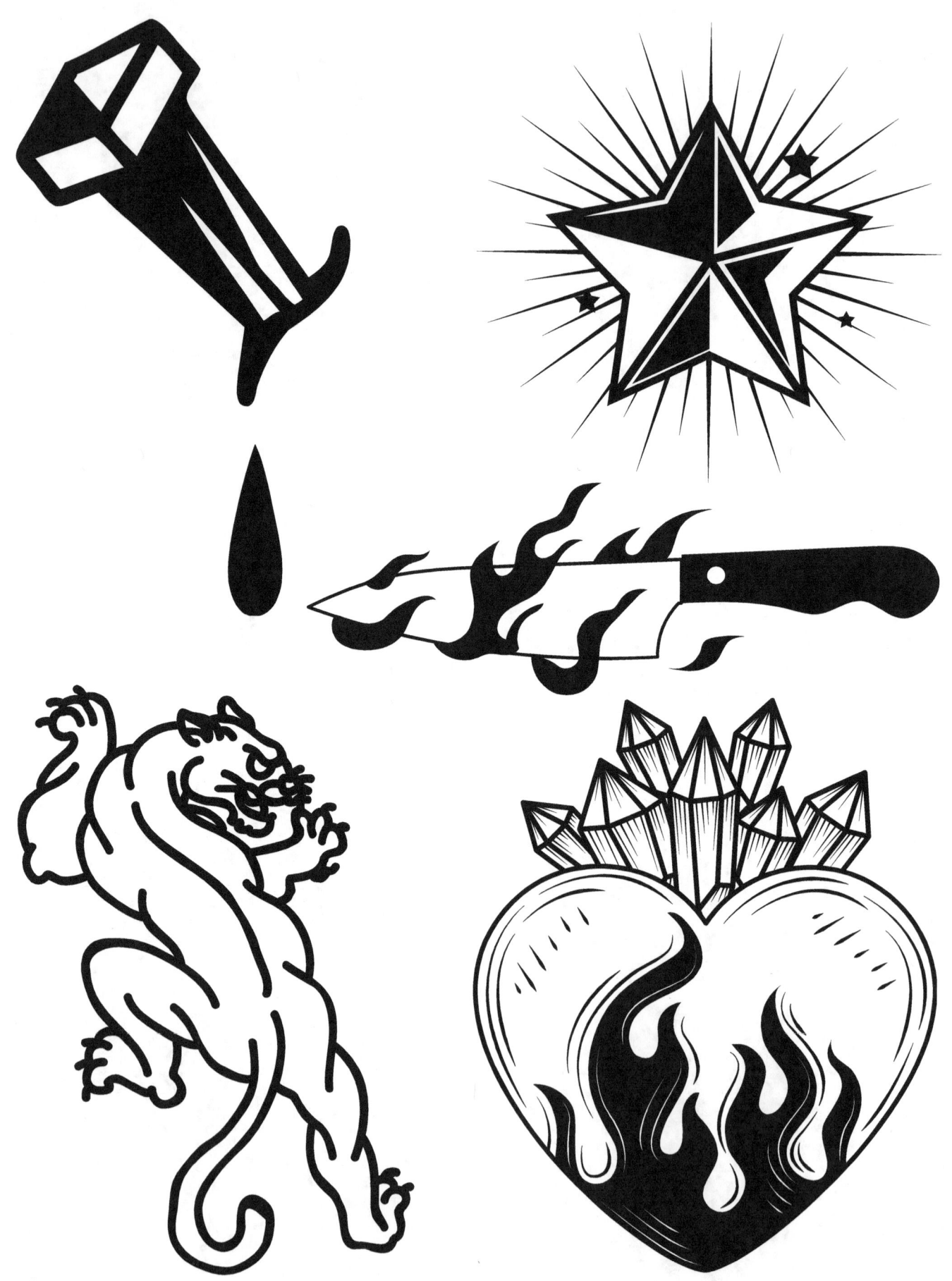

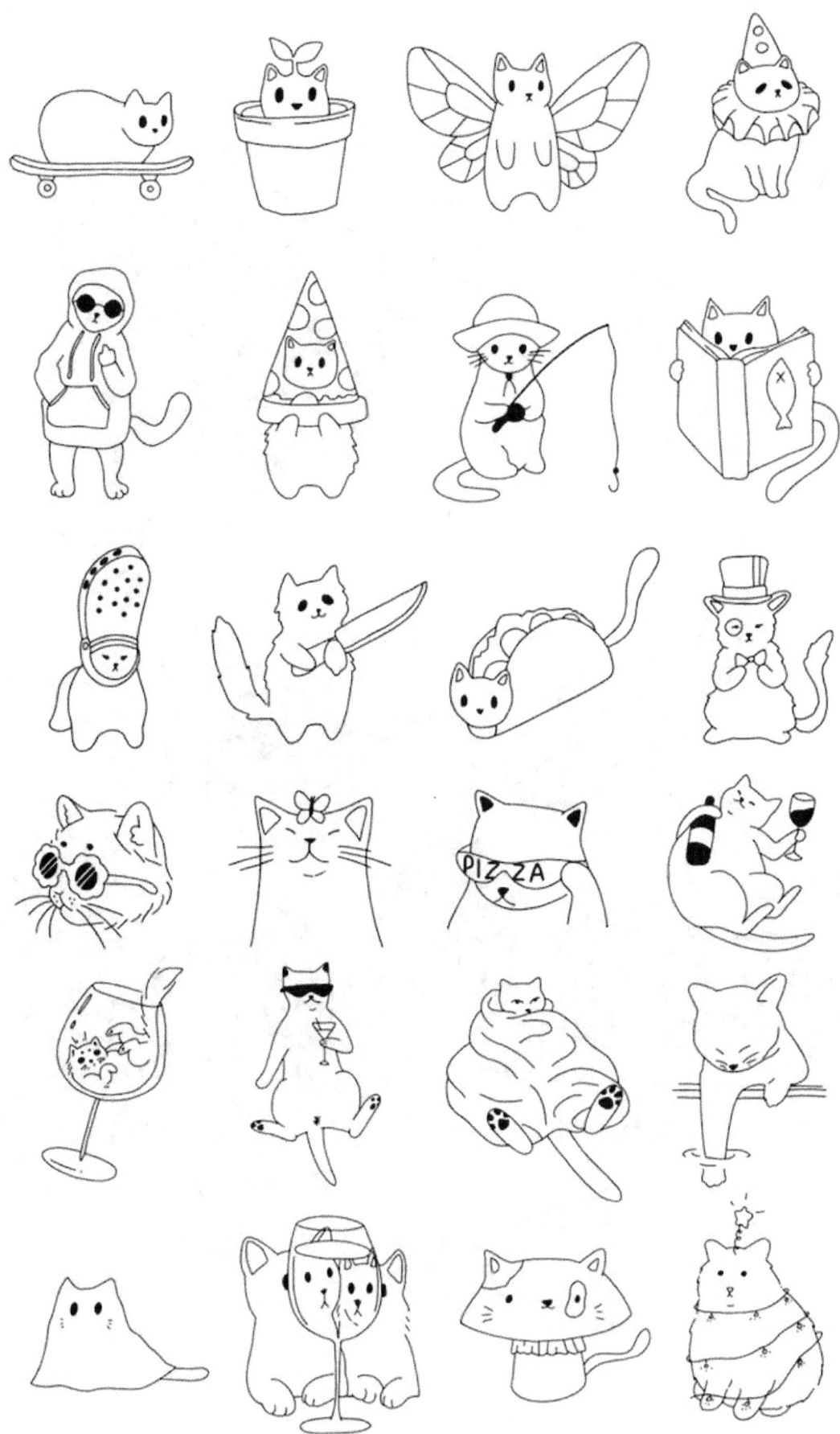

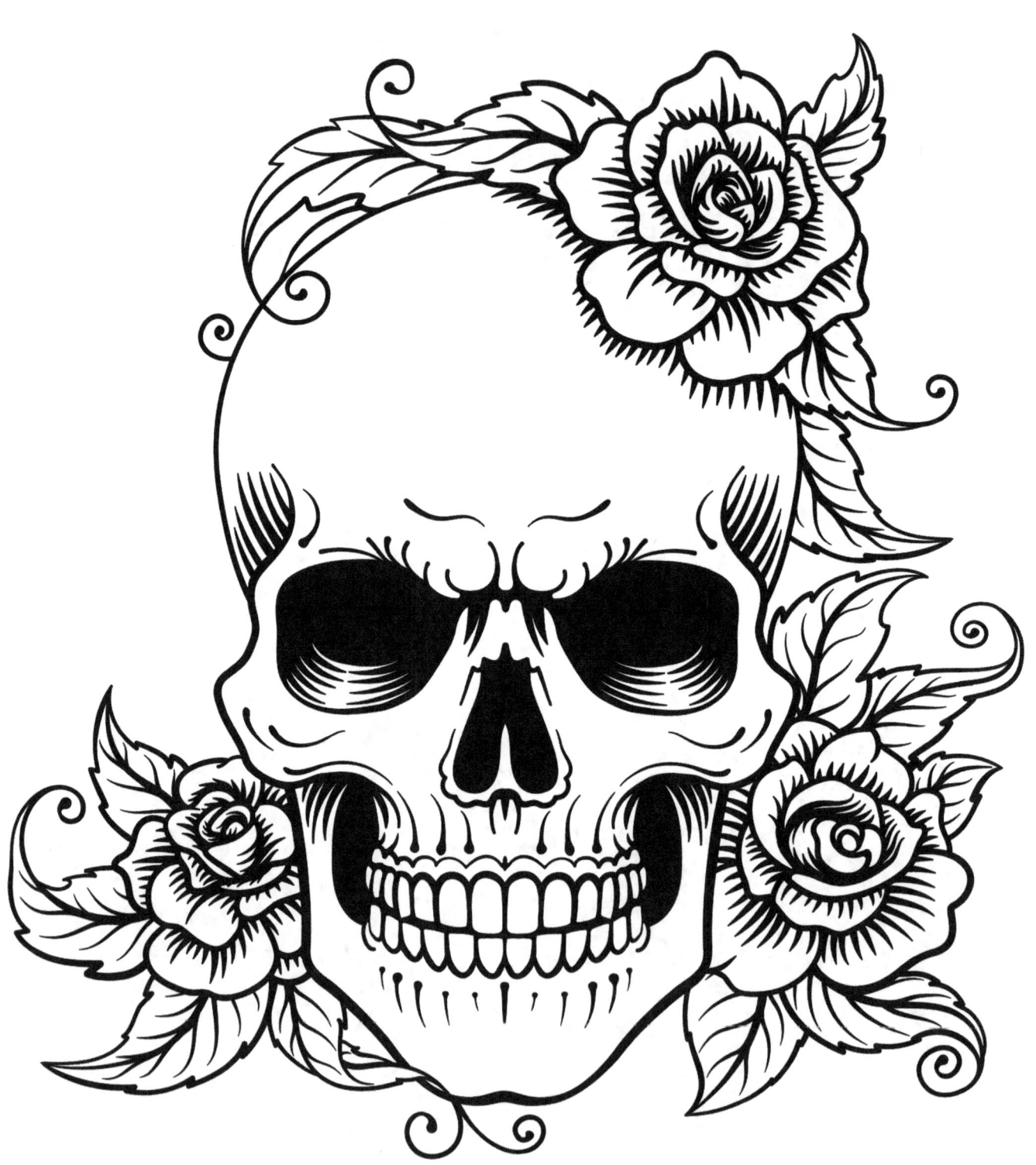

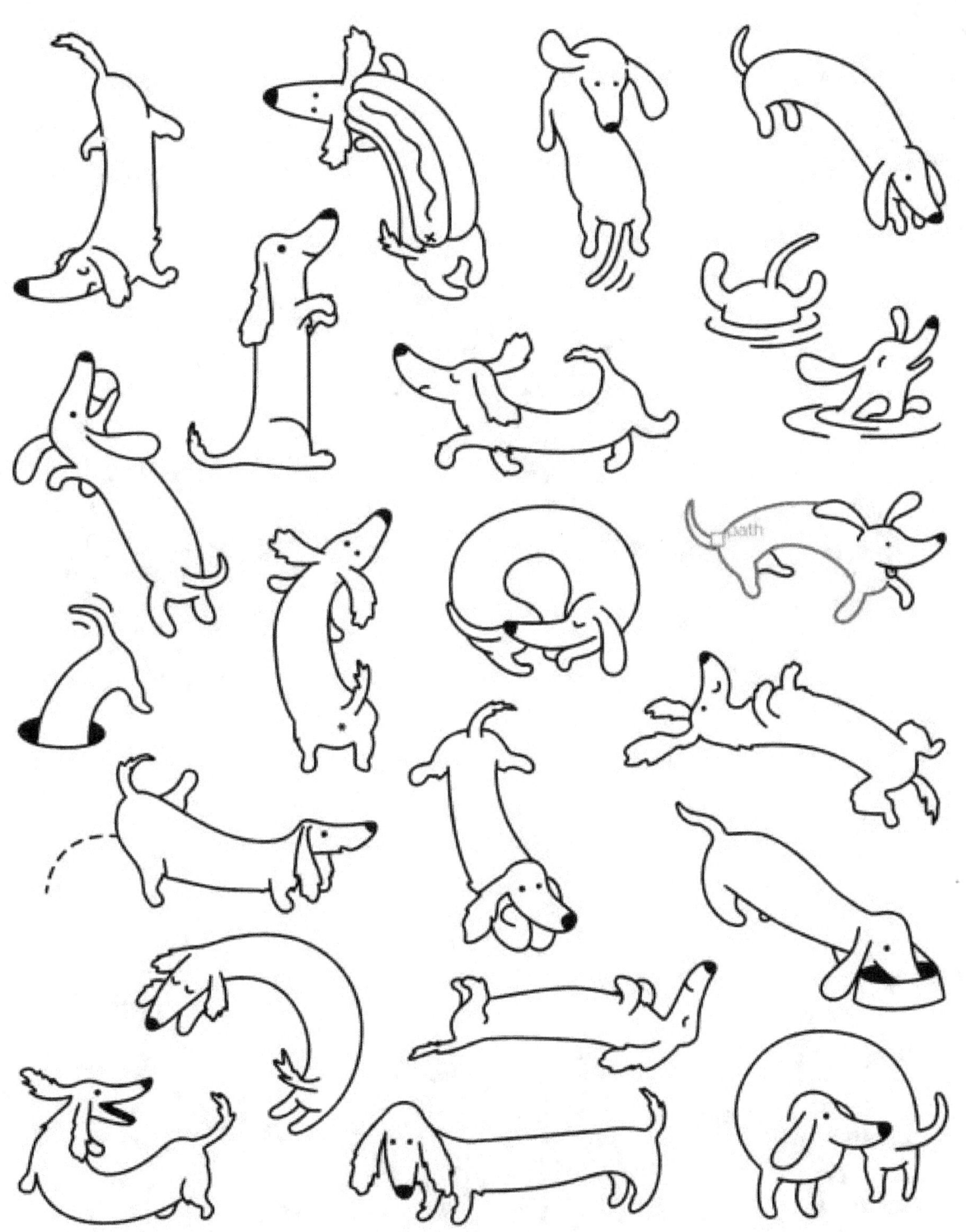

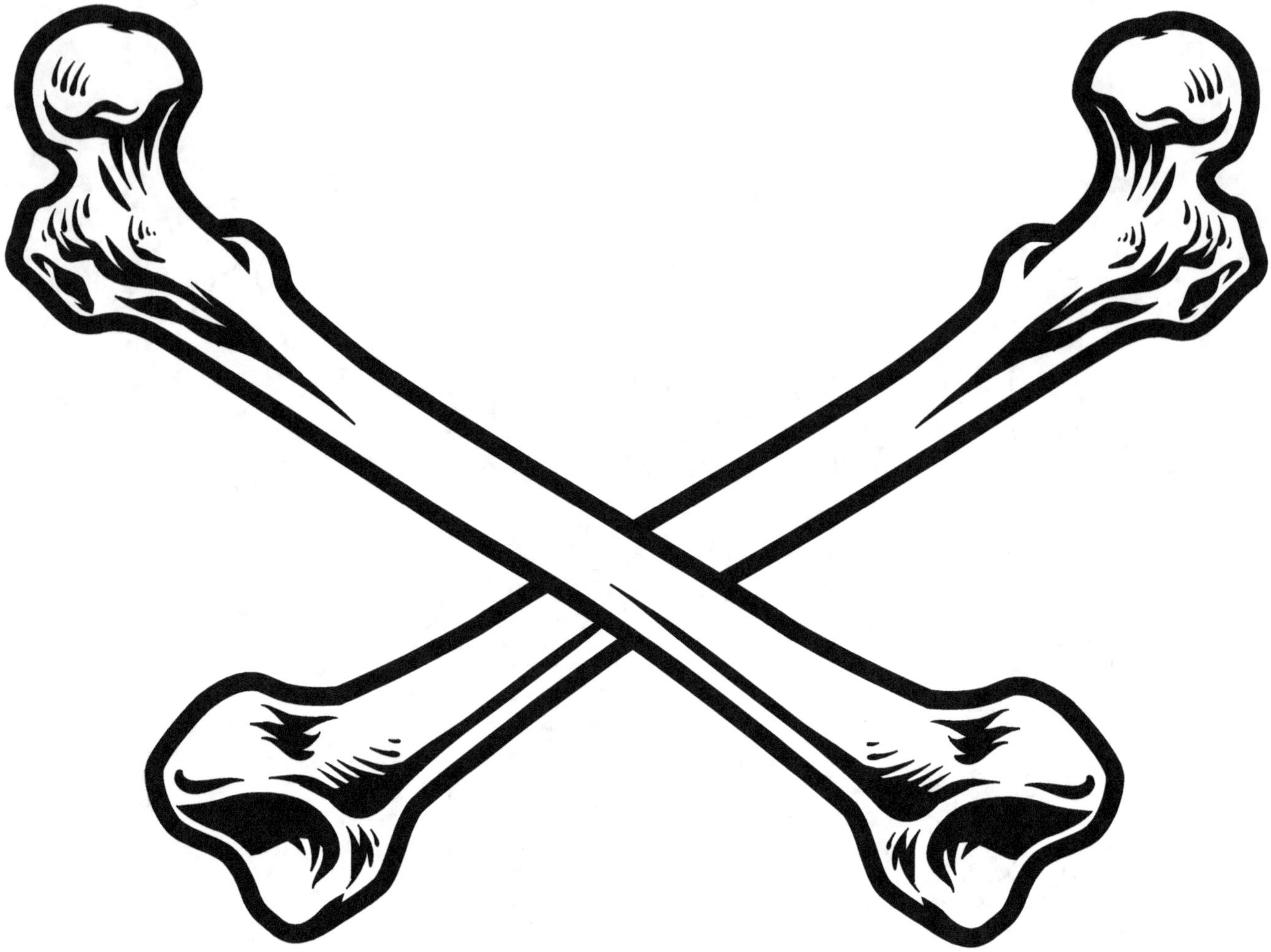

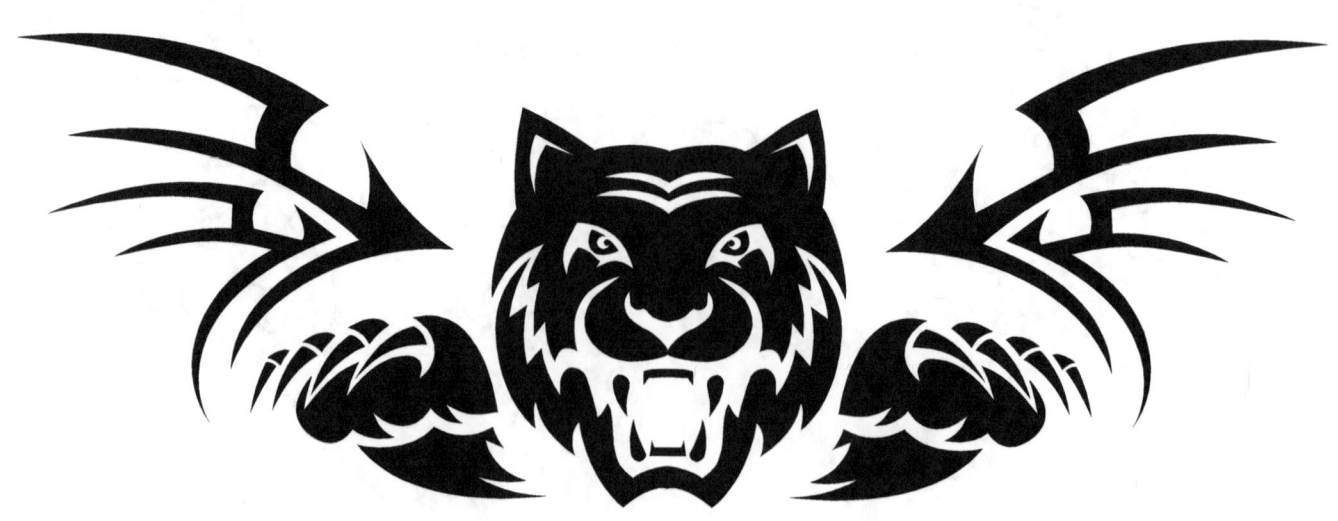

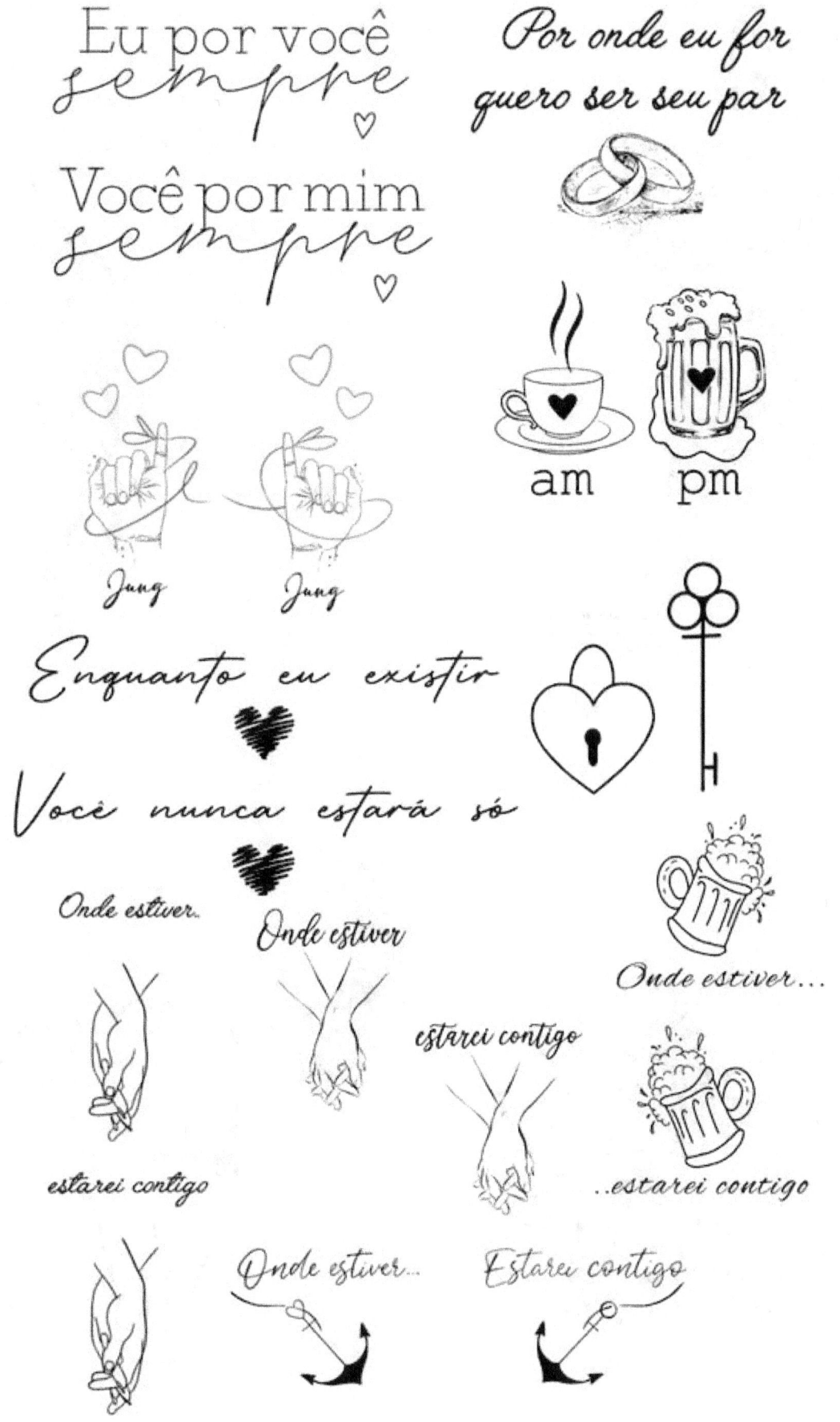

Eu por você
sempre ♡

Você por mim
sempre ♡

Por onde eu for
quero ser seu par

Jung   *Jung*

am   pm

Enquanto eu existir ♥

Você nunca estará só ♥

Onde estiver.

estarei contigo

Onde estiver

estarei contigo

Onde estiver...

..estarei contigo

Onde estiver...   Estarei contigo

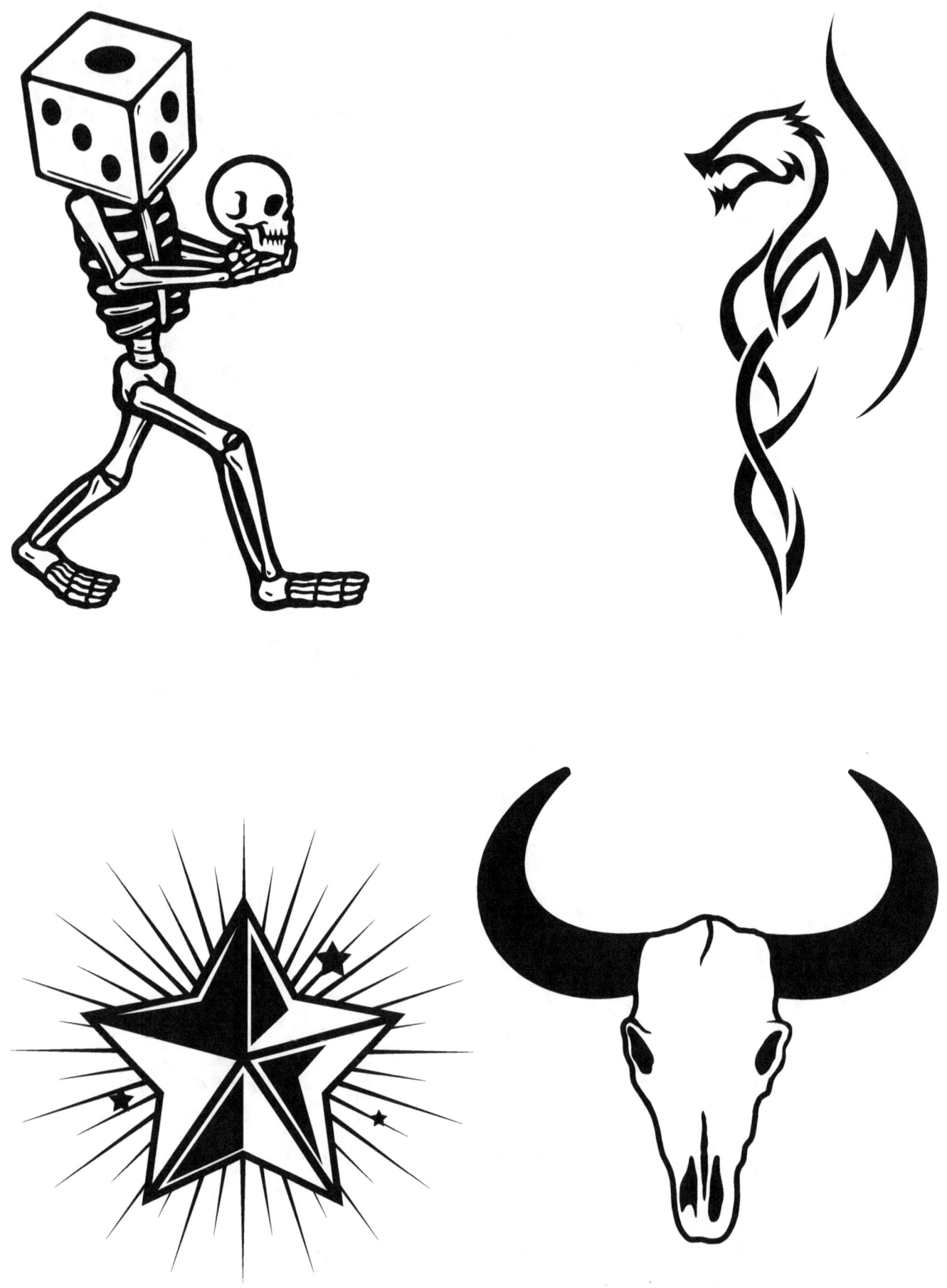

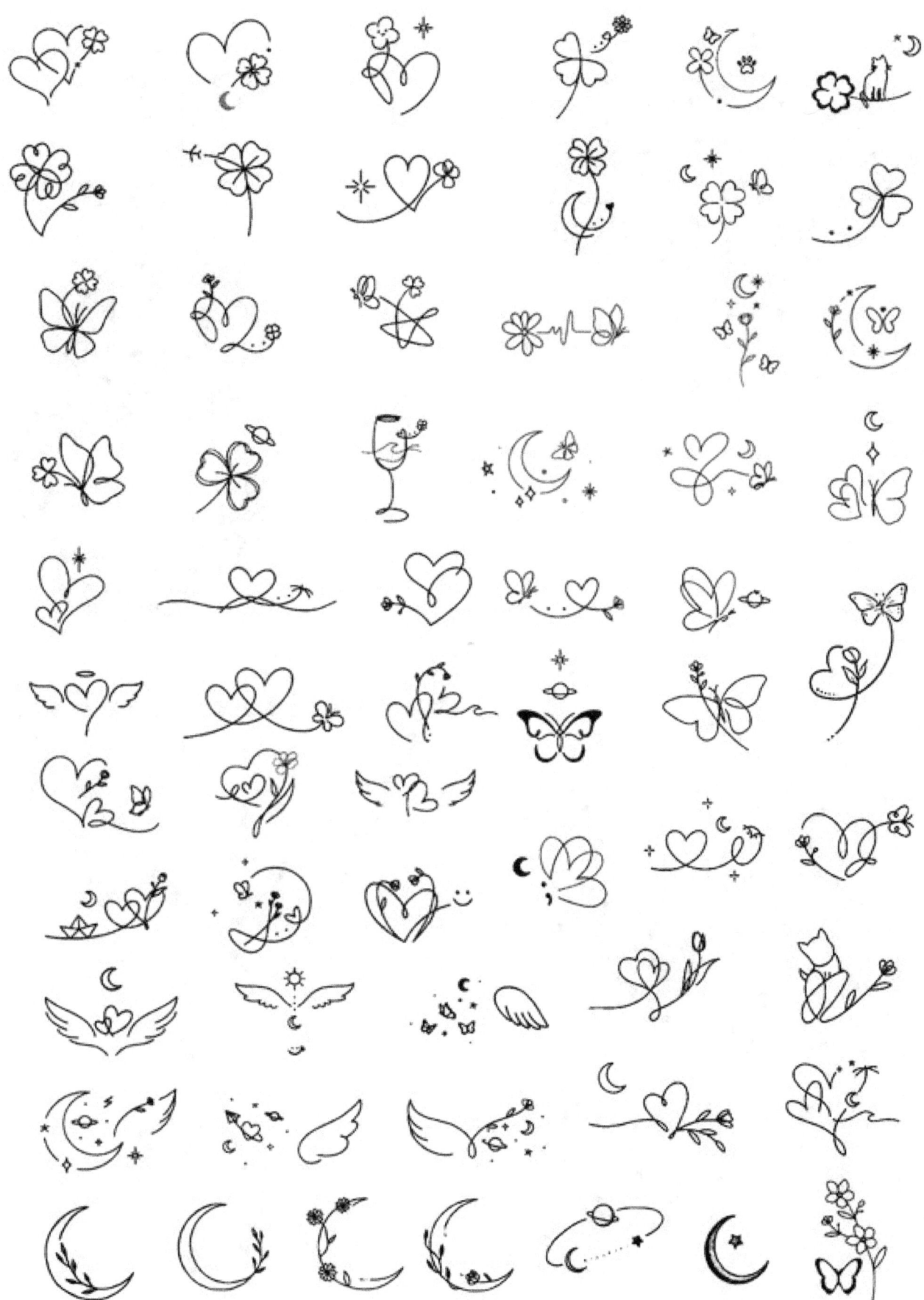

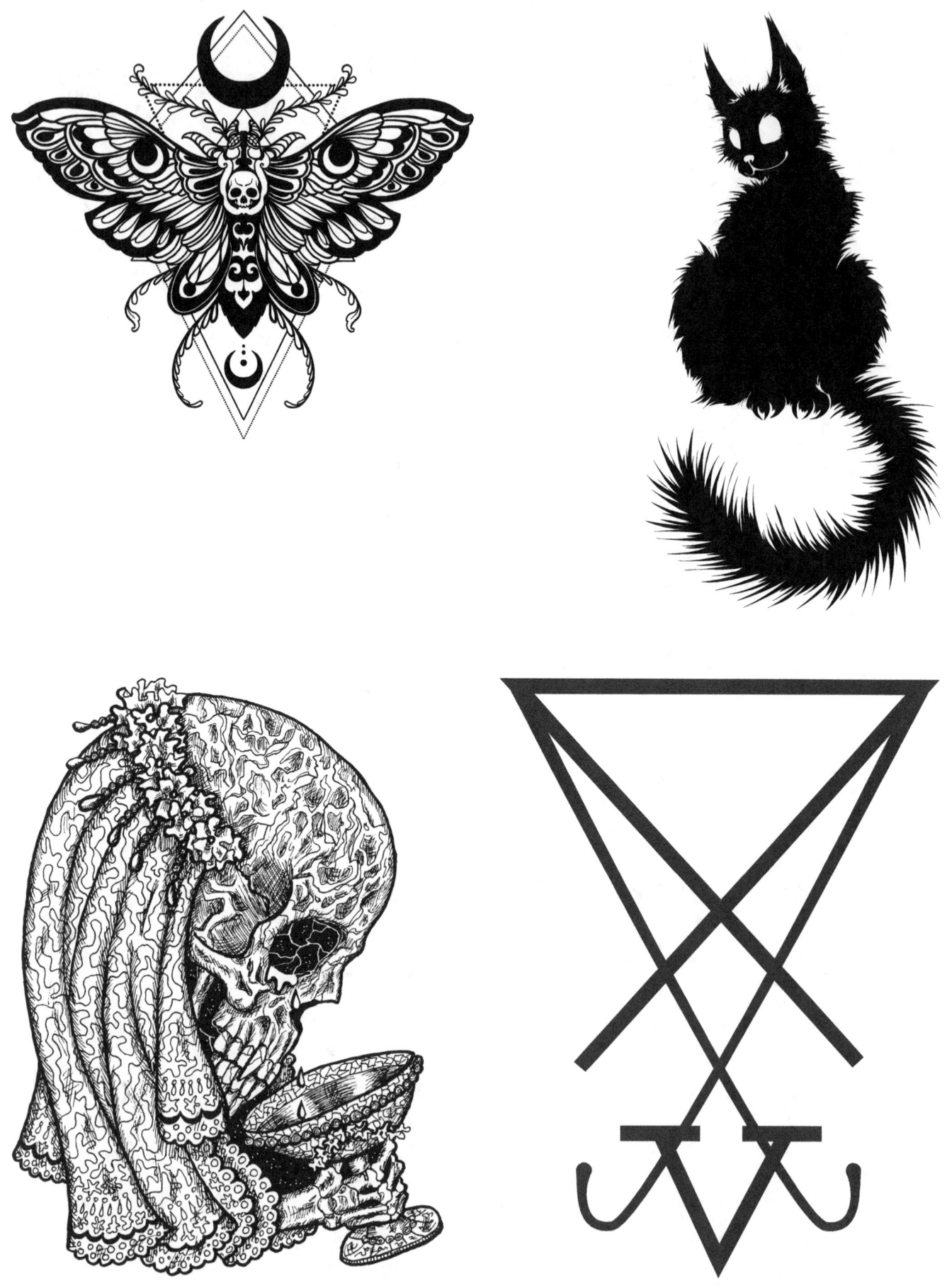

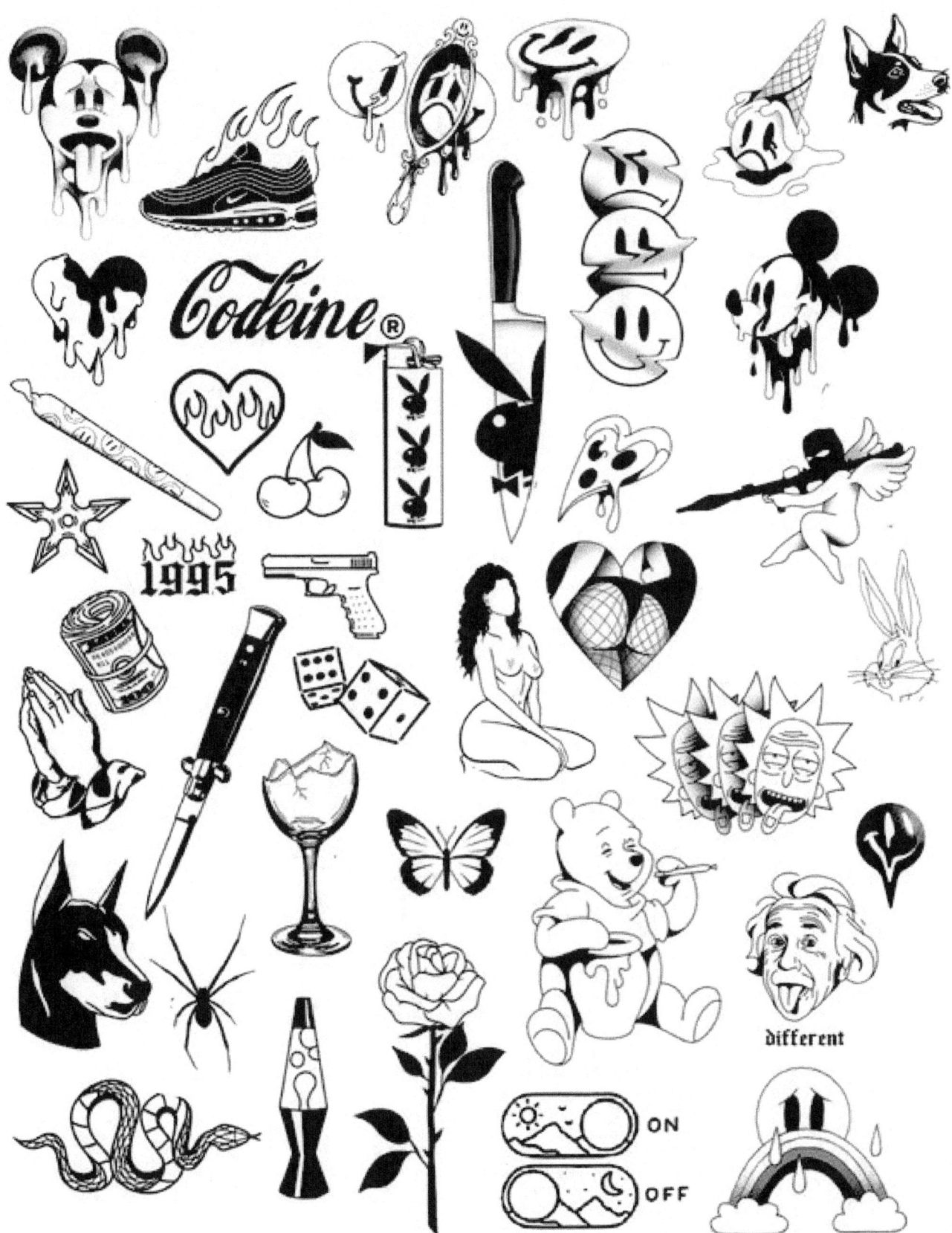

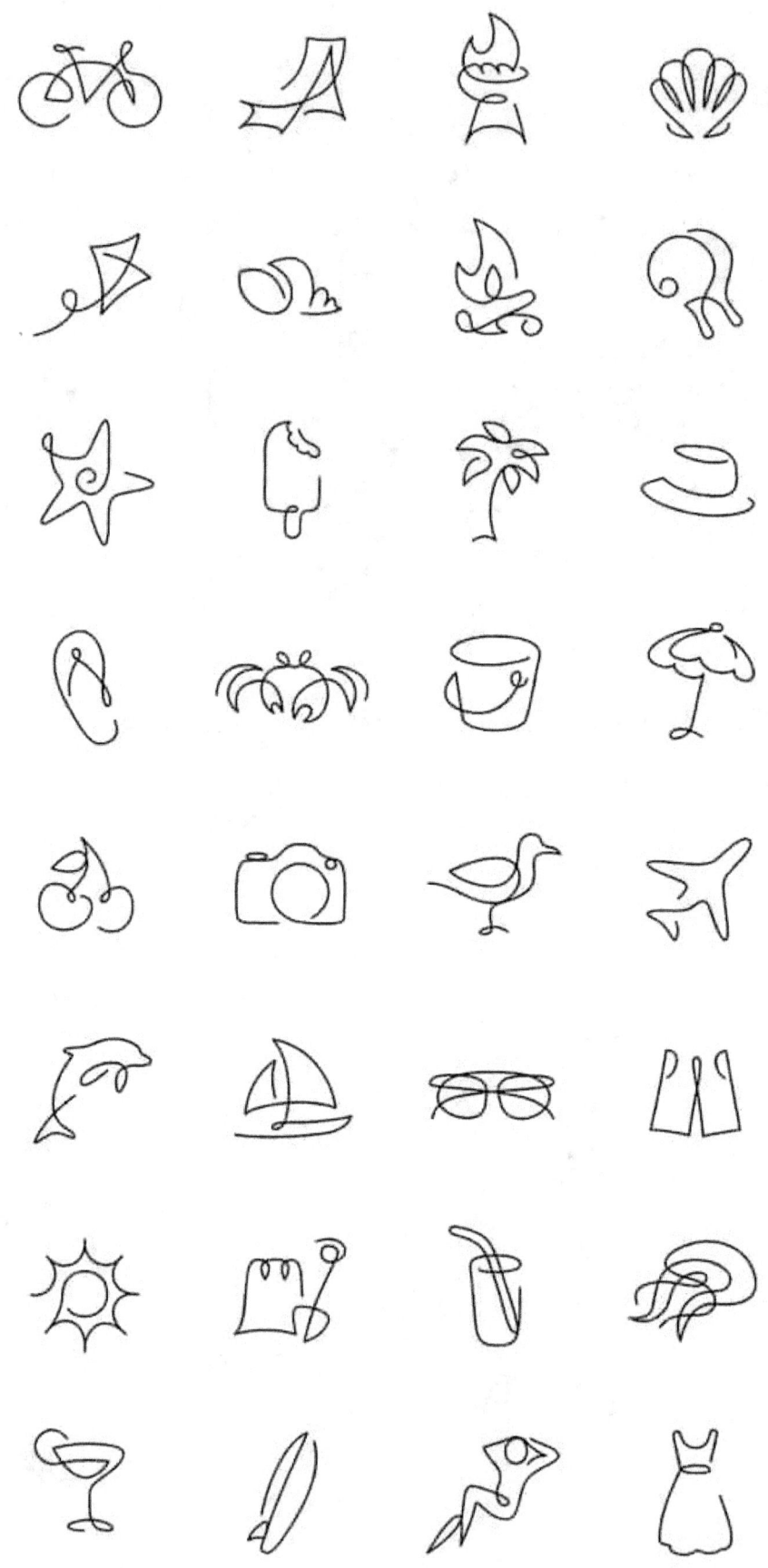

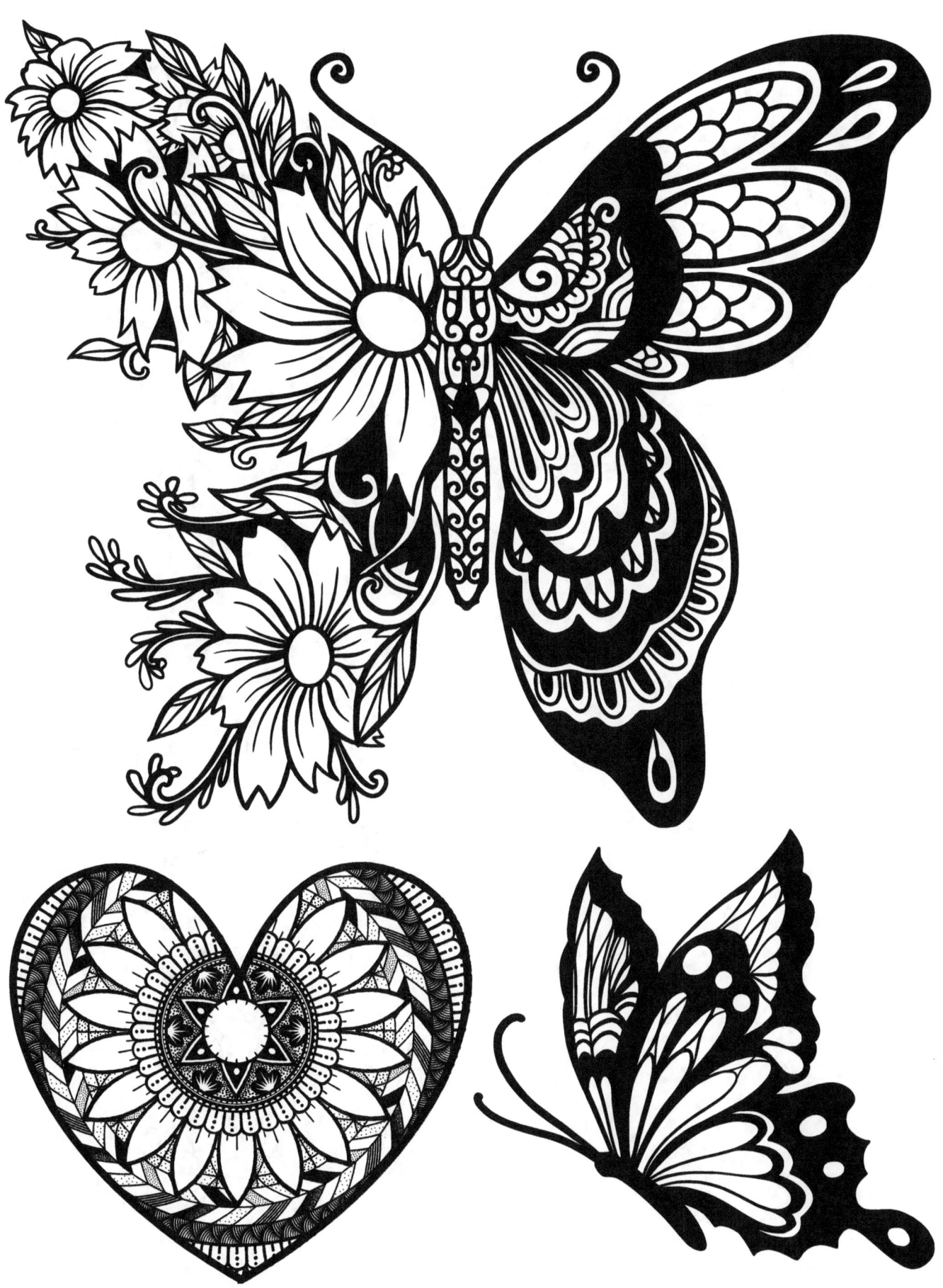

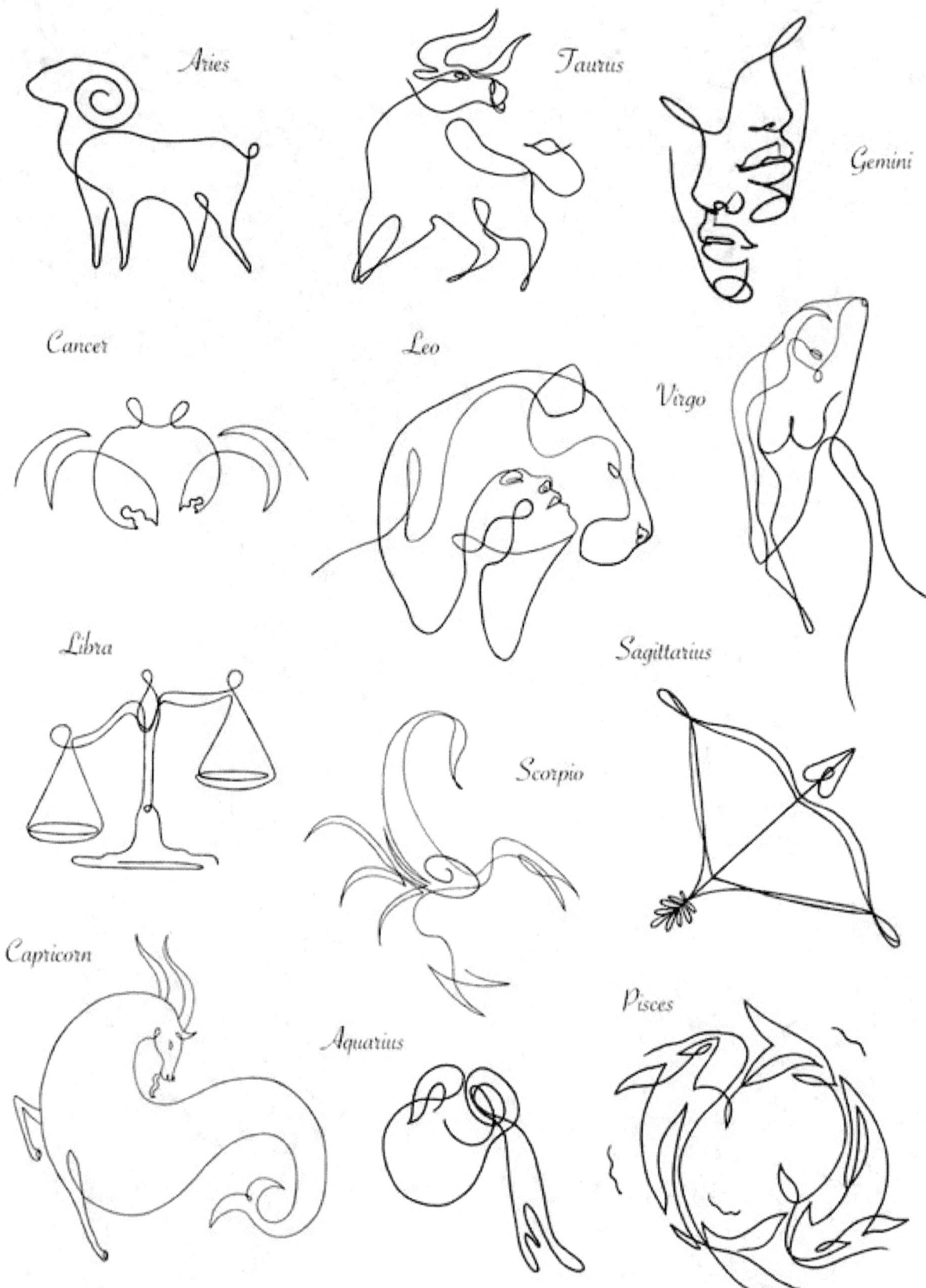

Aries

Taurus

Gemini

Cancer

Leo

Virgo

Libra

Scorpio

Sagittarius

Capricorn

Aquarius

Pisces

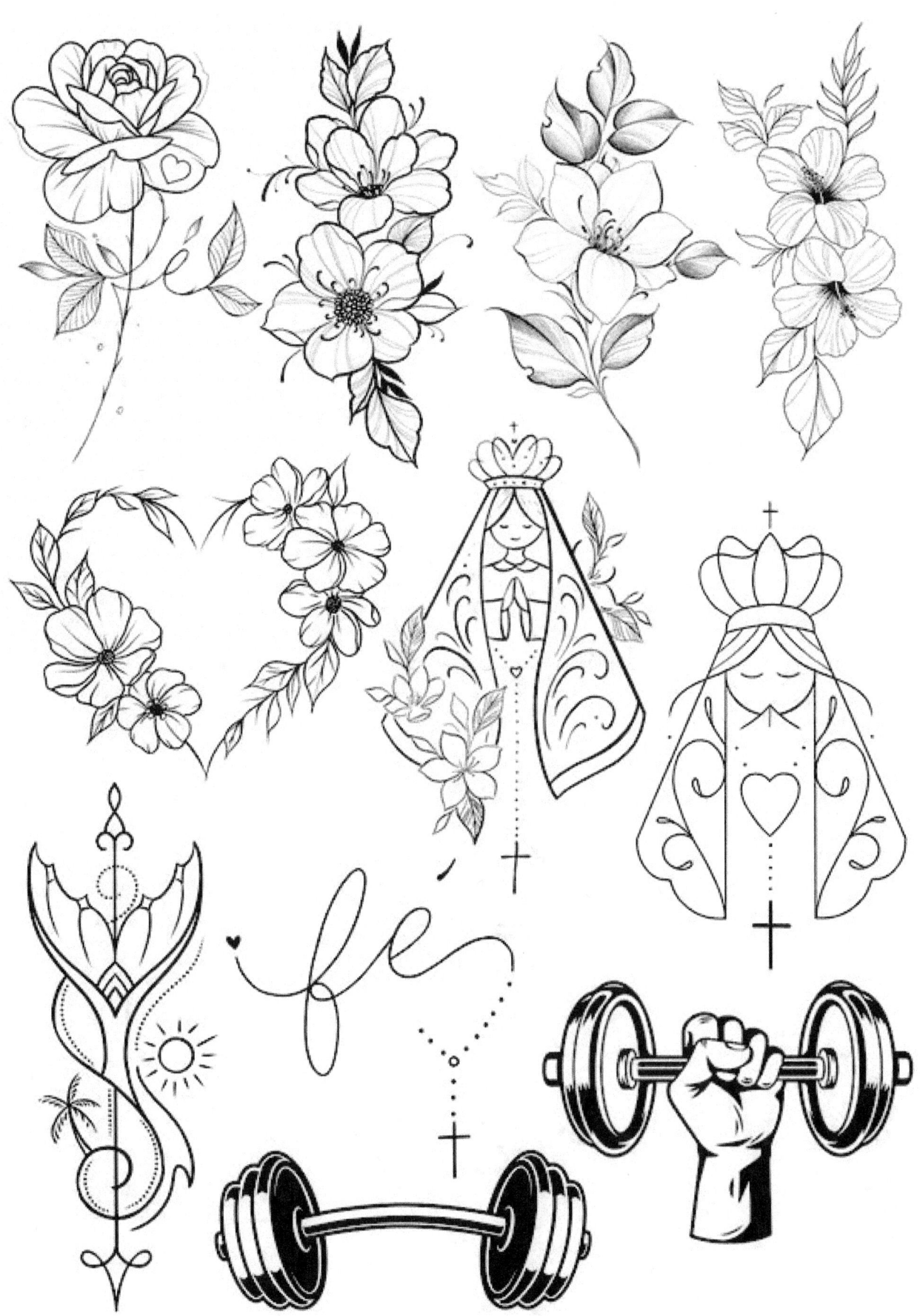

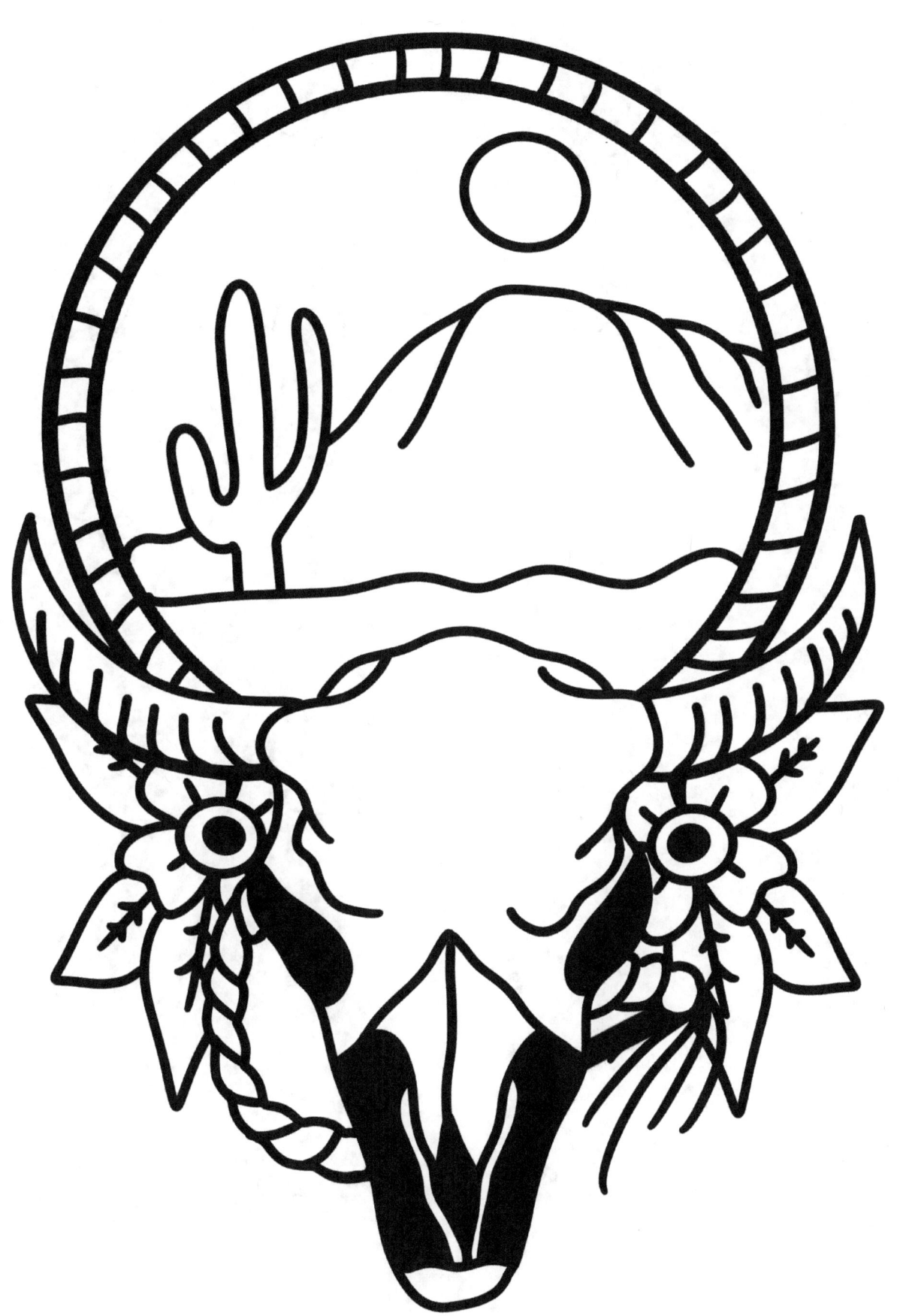

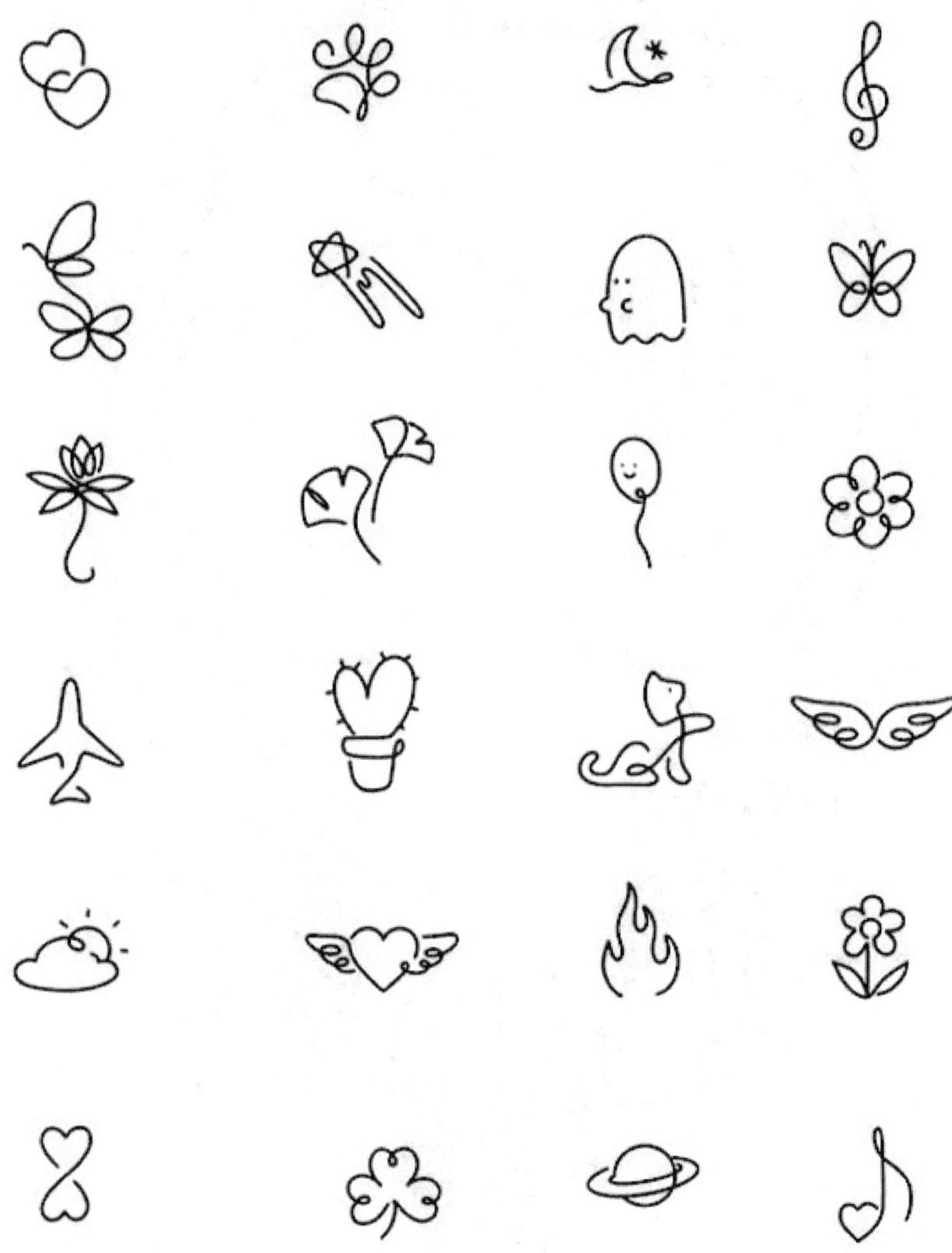

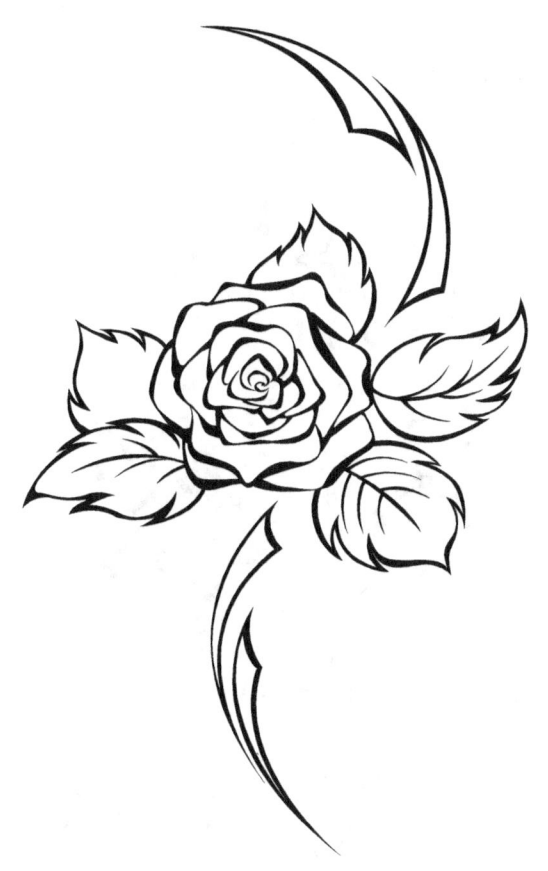

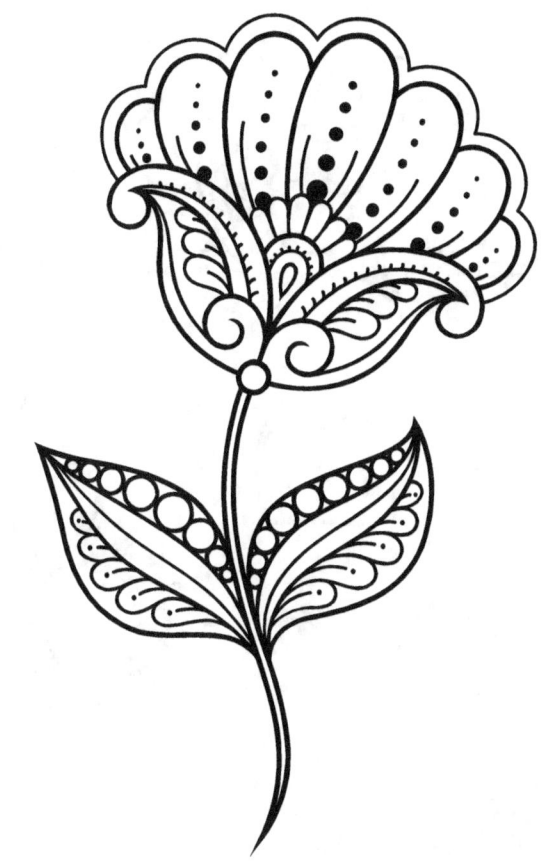

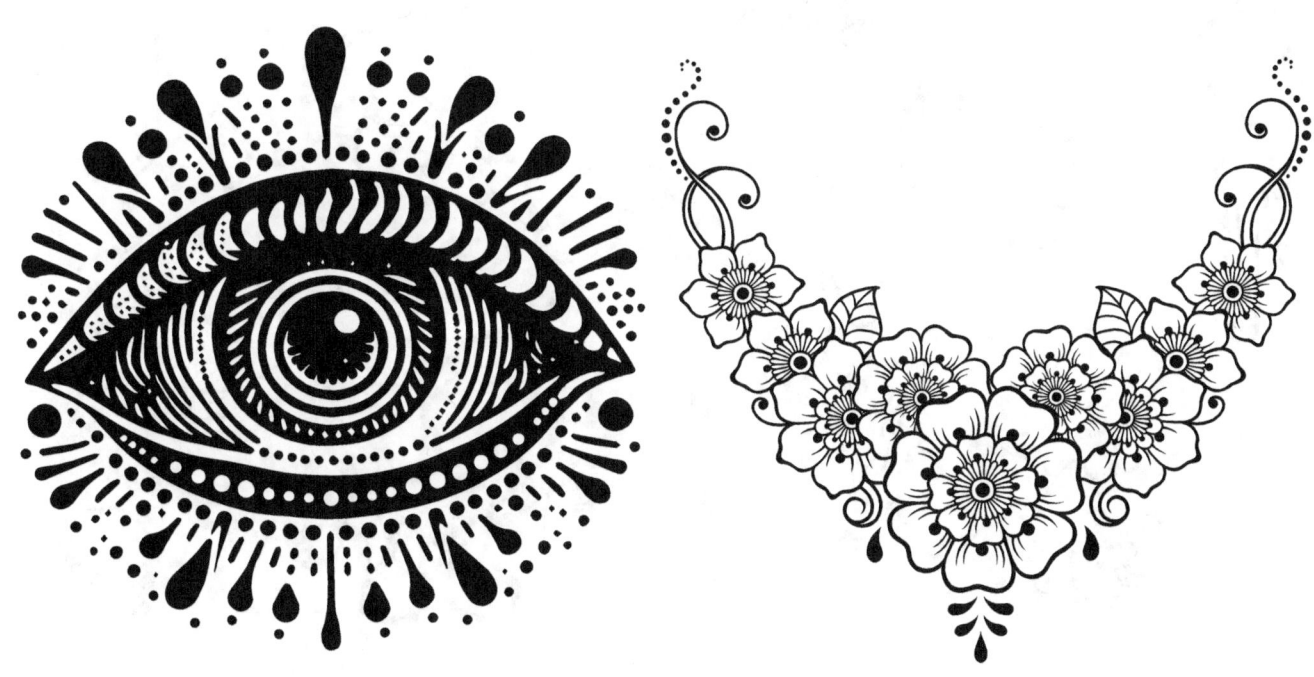

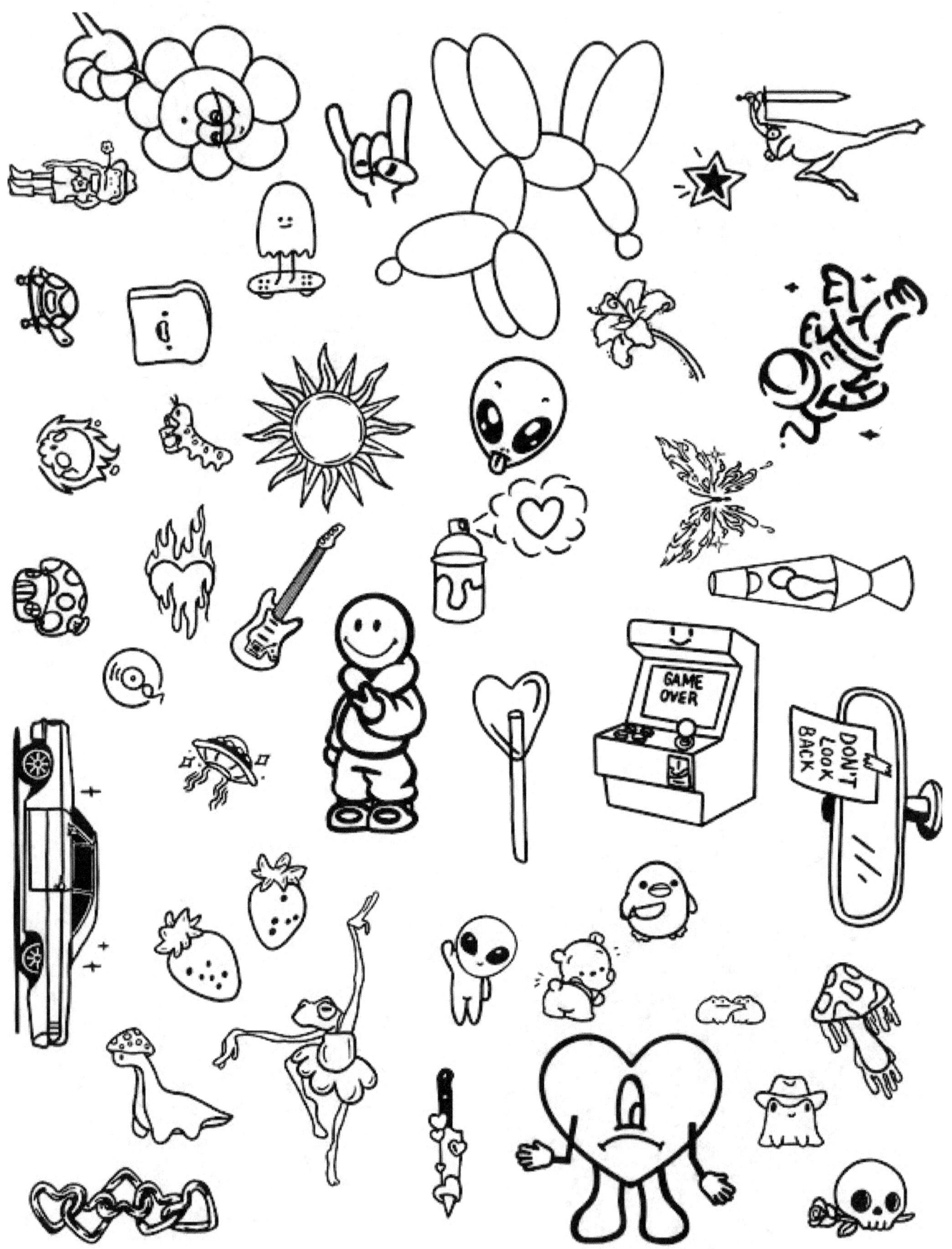

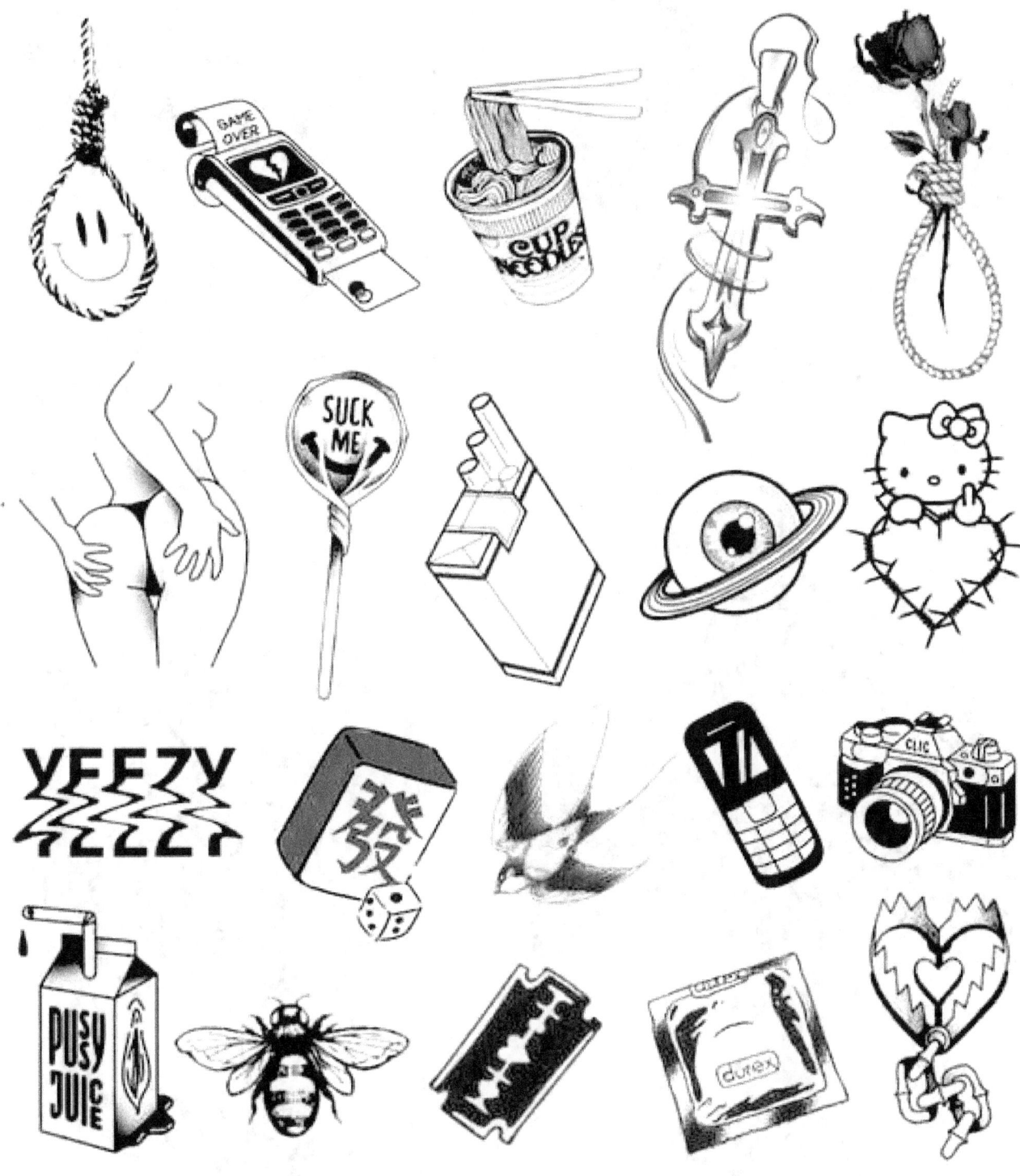

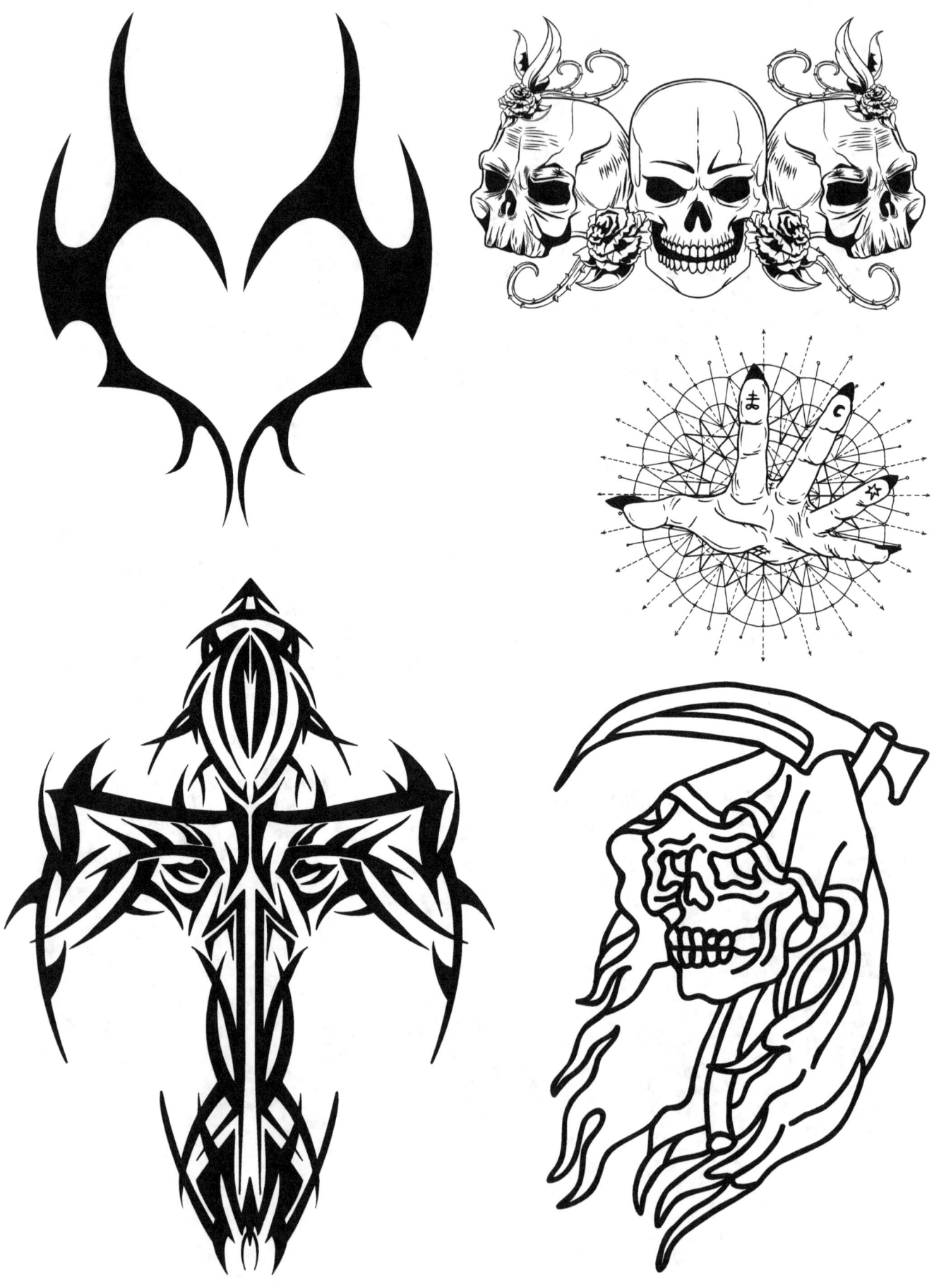

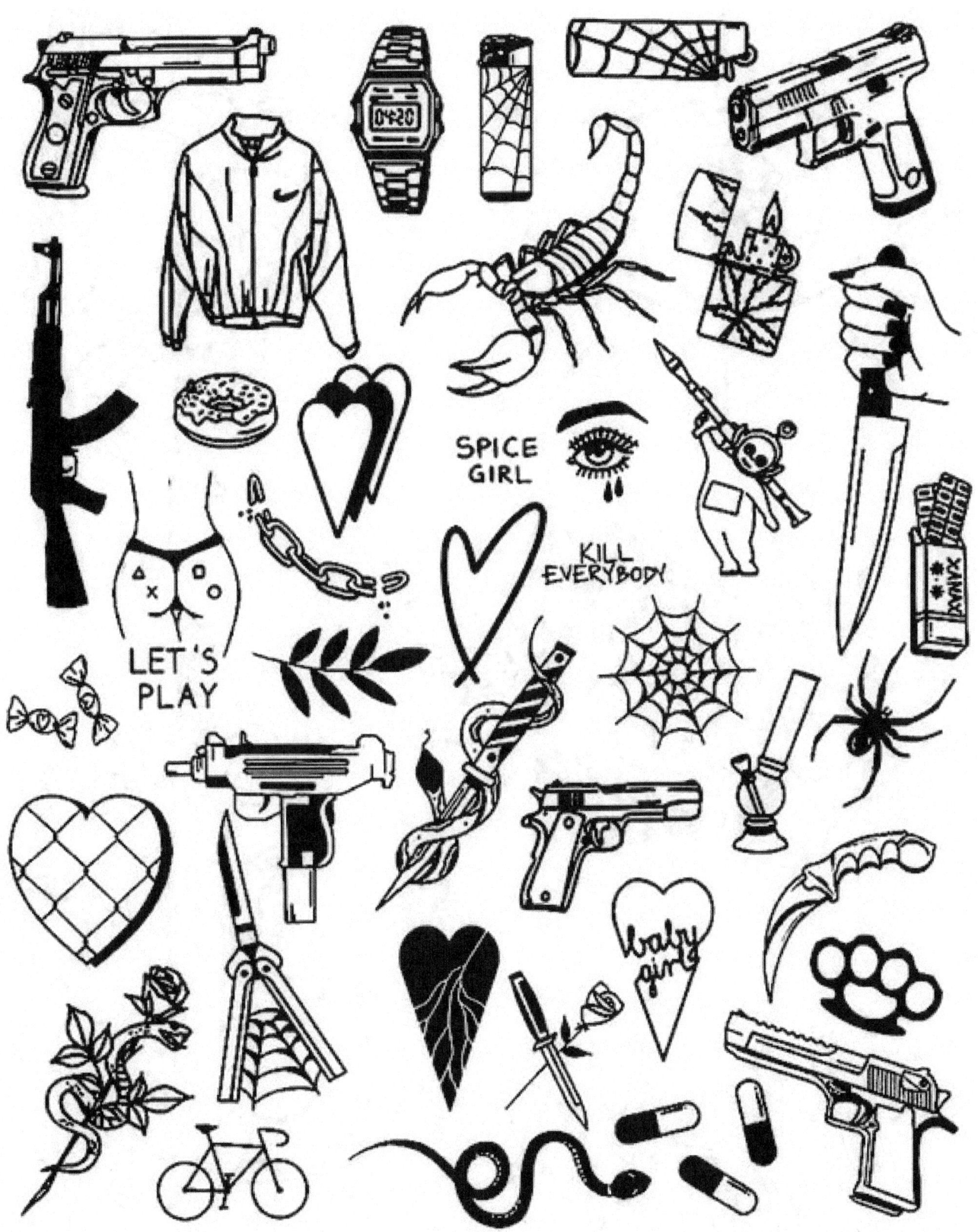

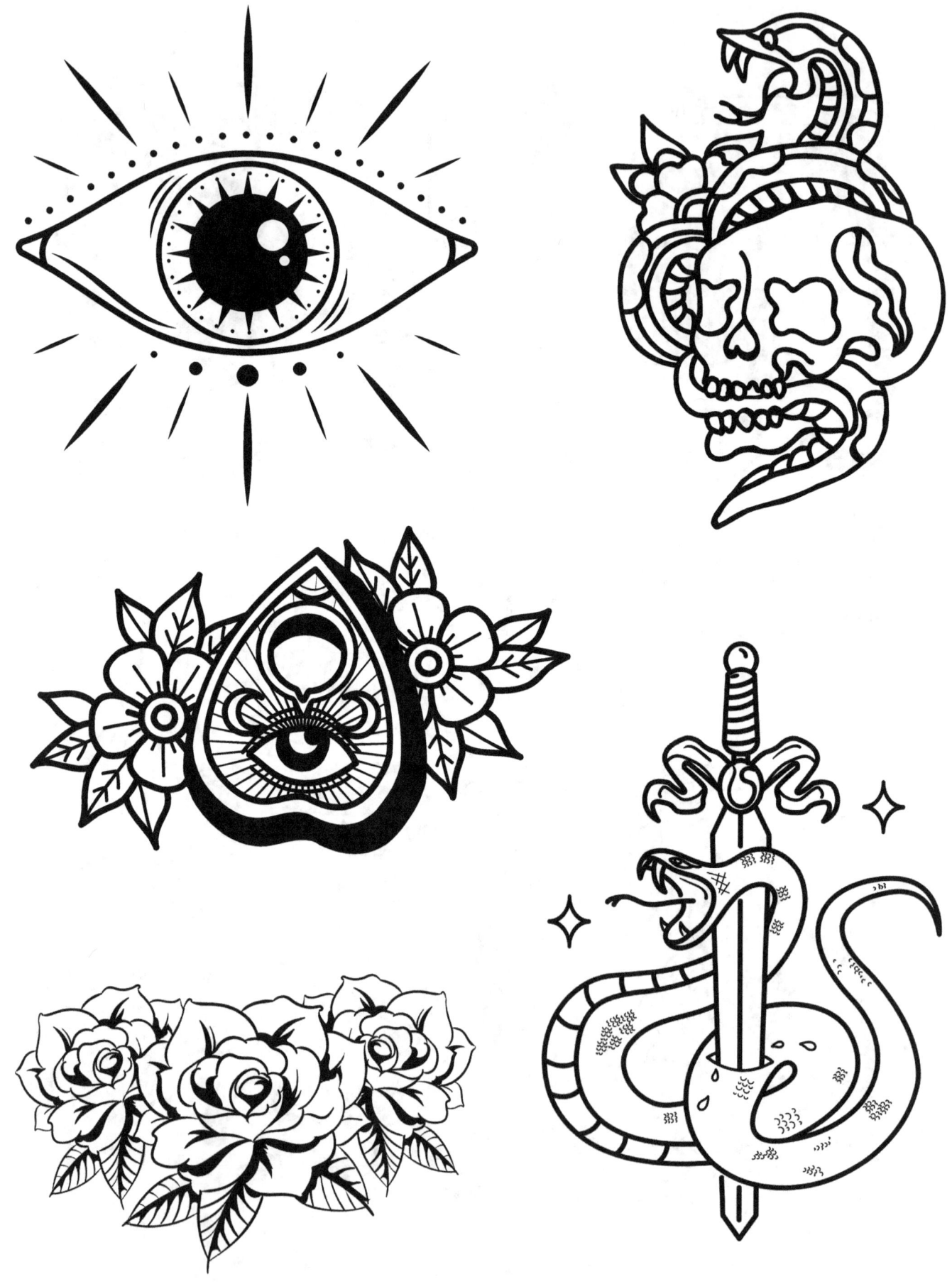

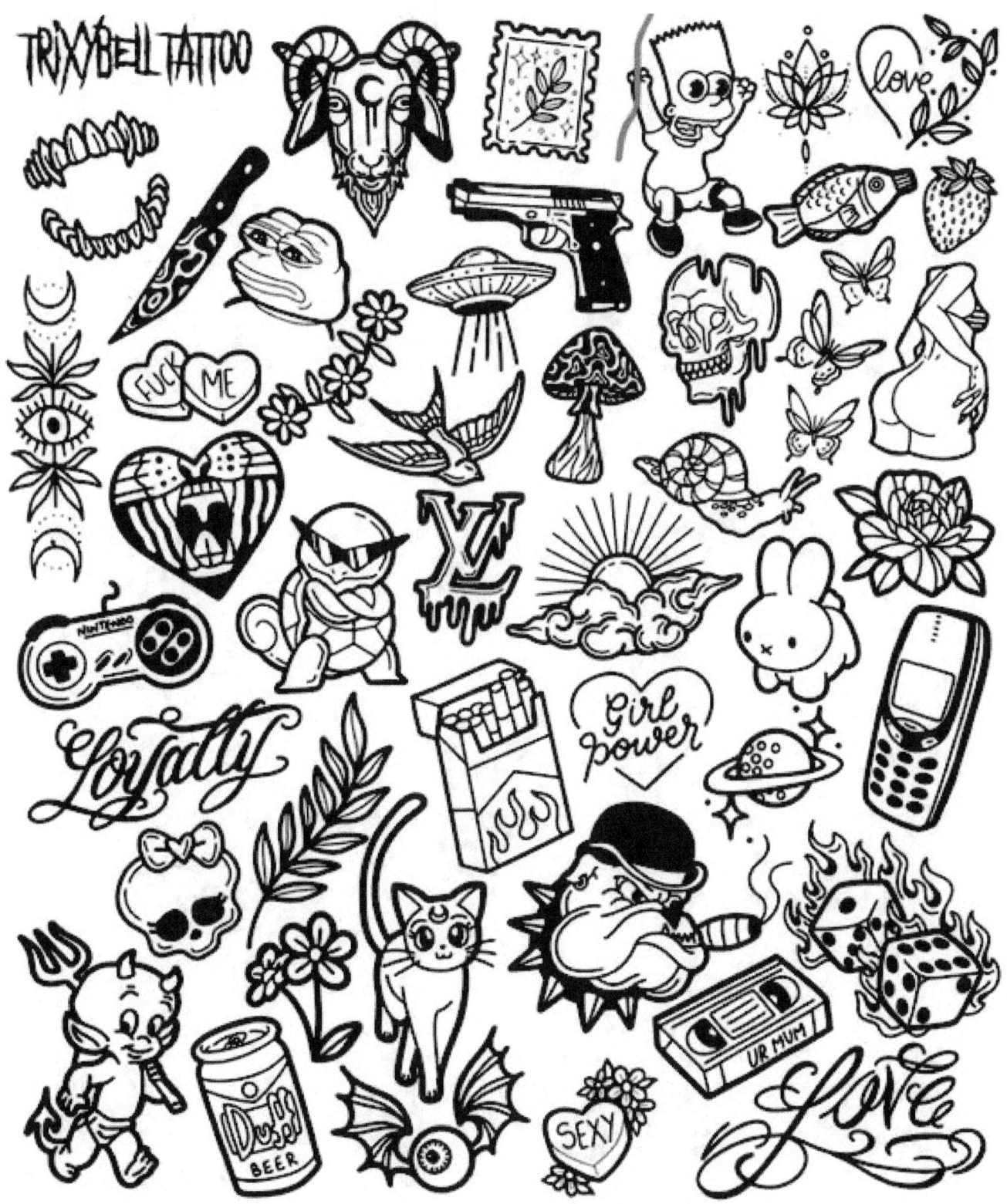

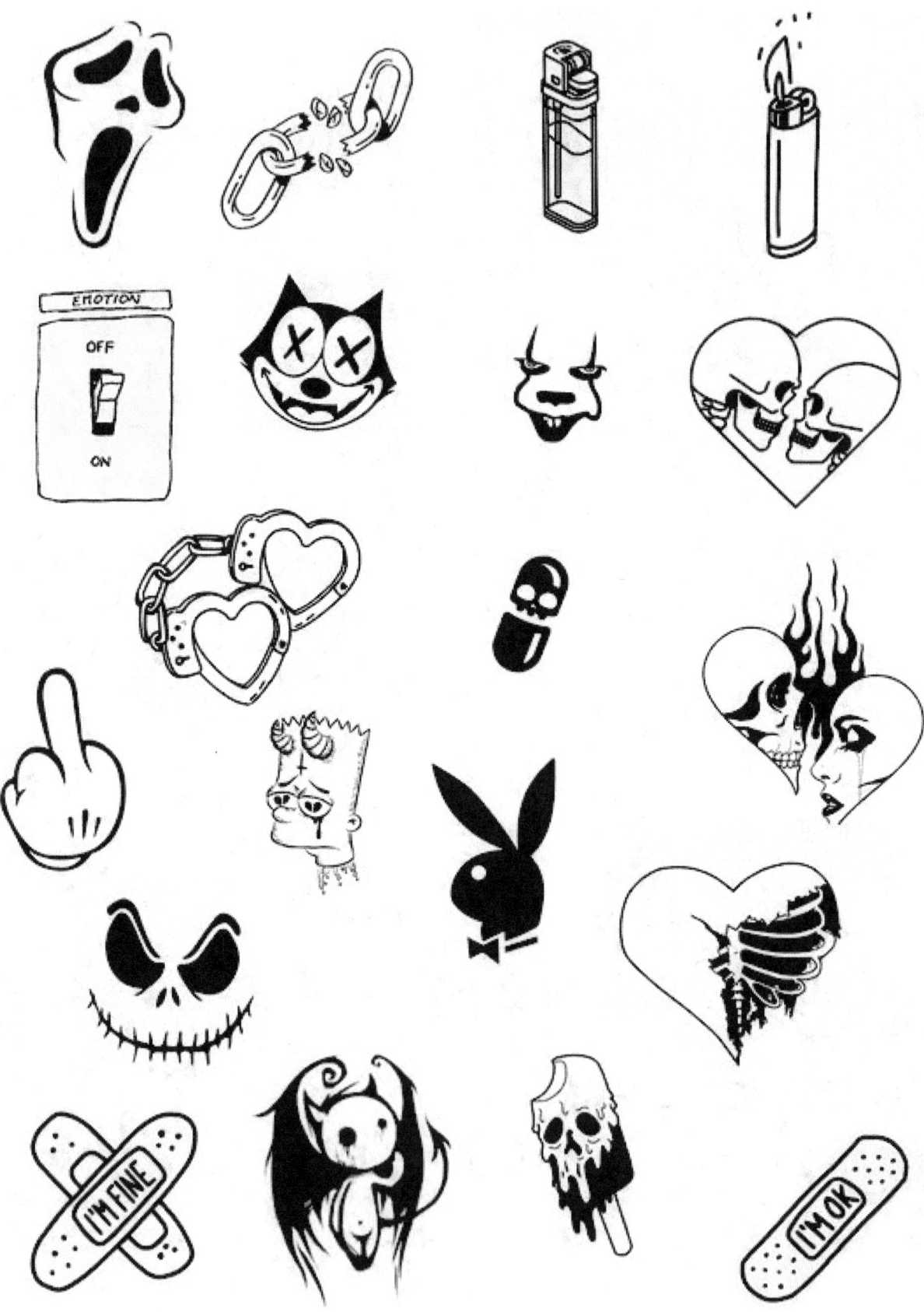

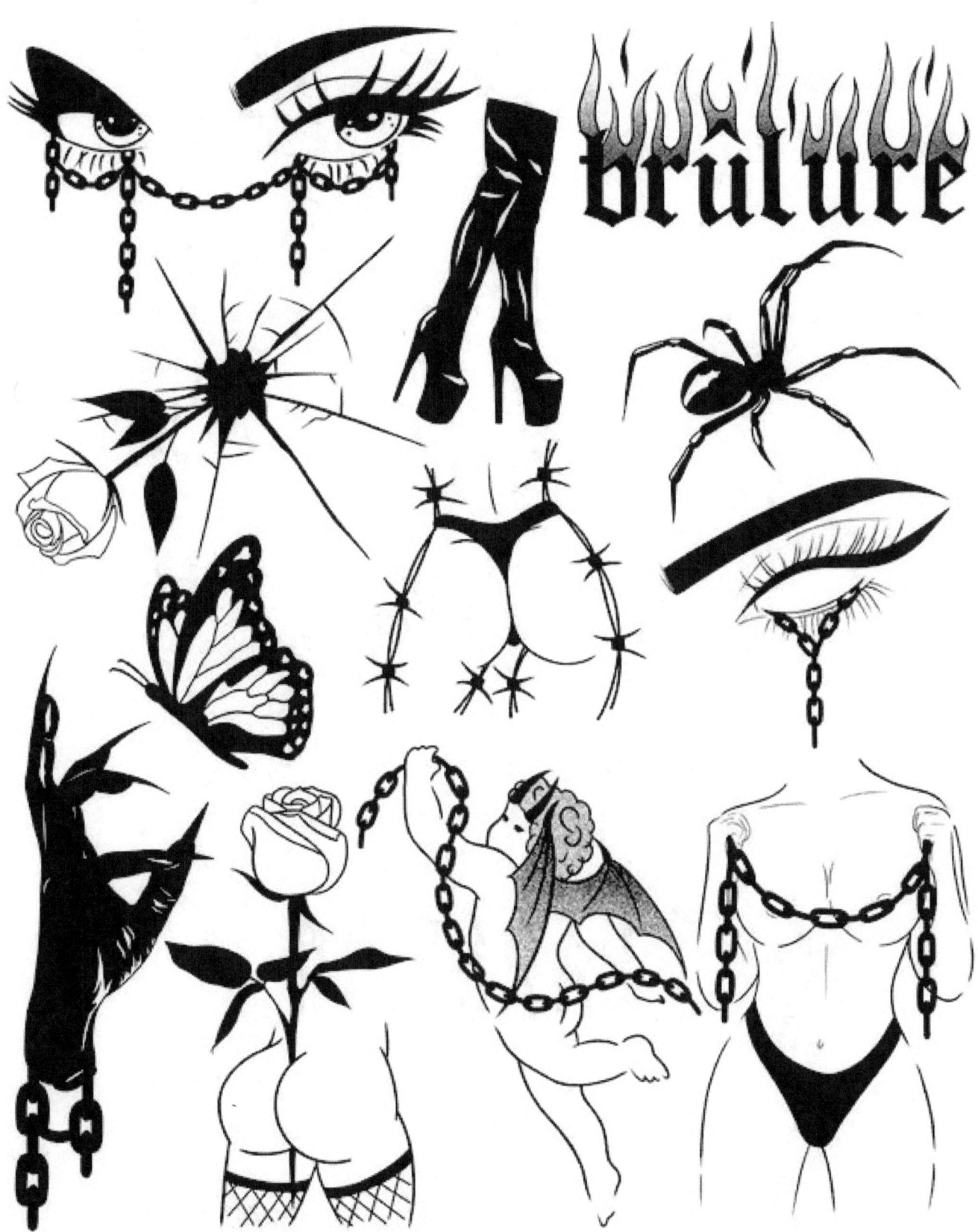

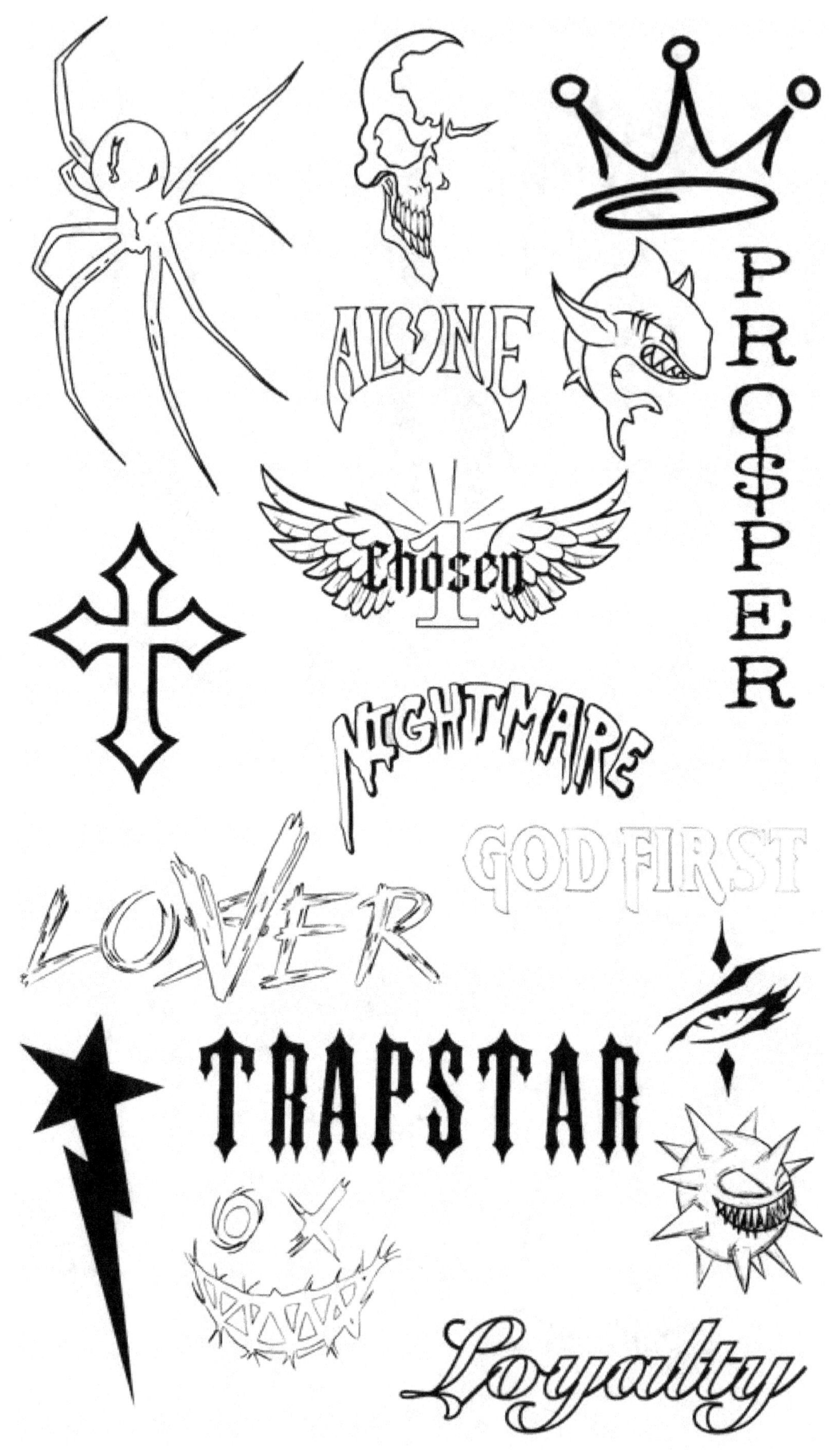

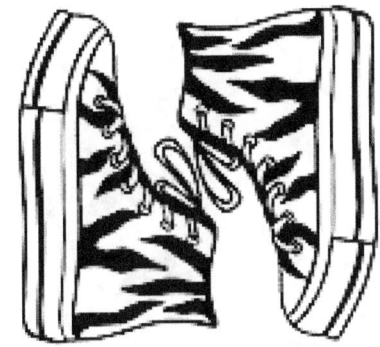

Deadline

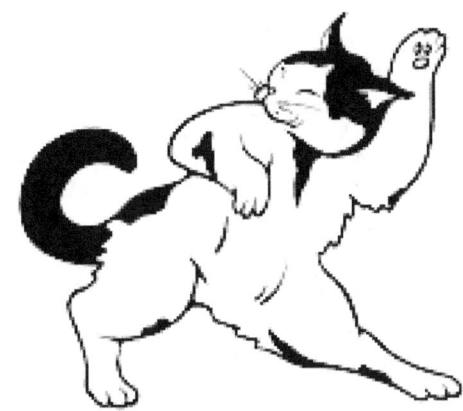

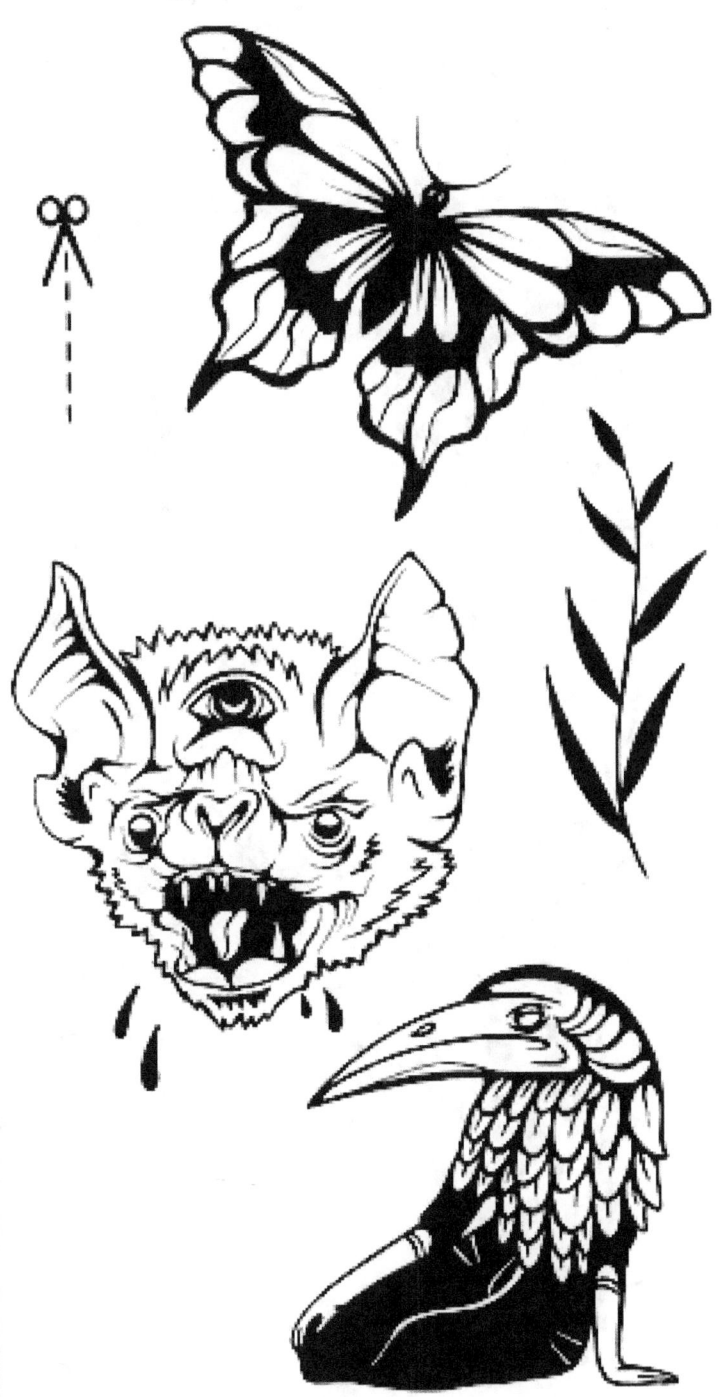

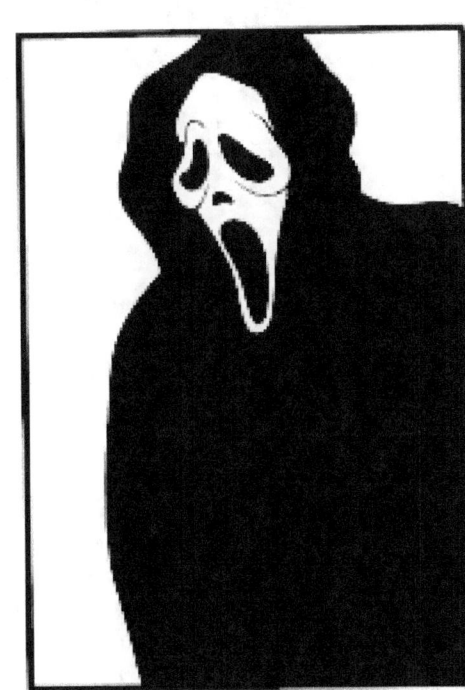

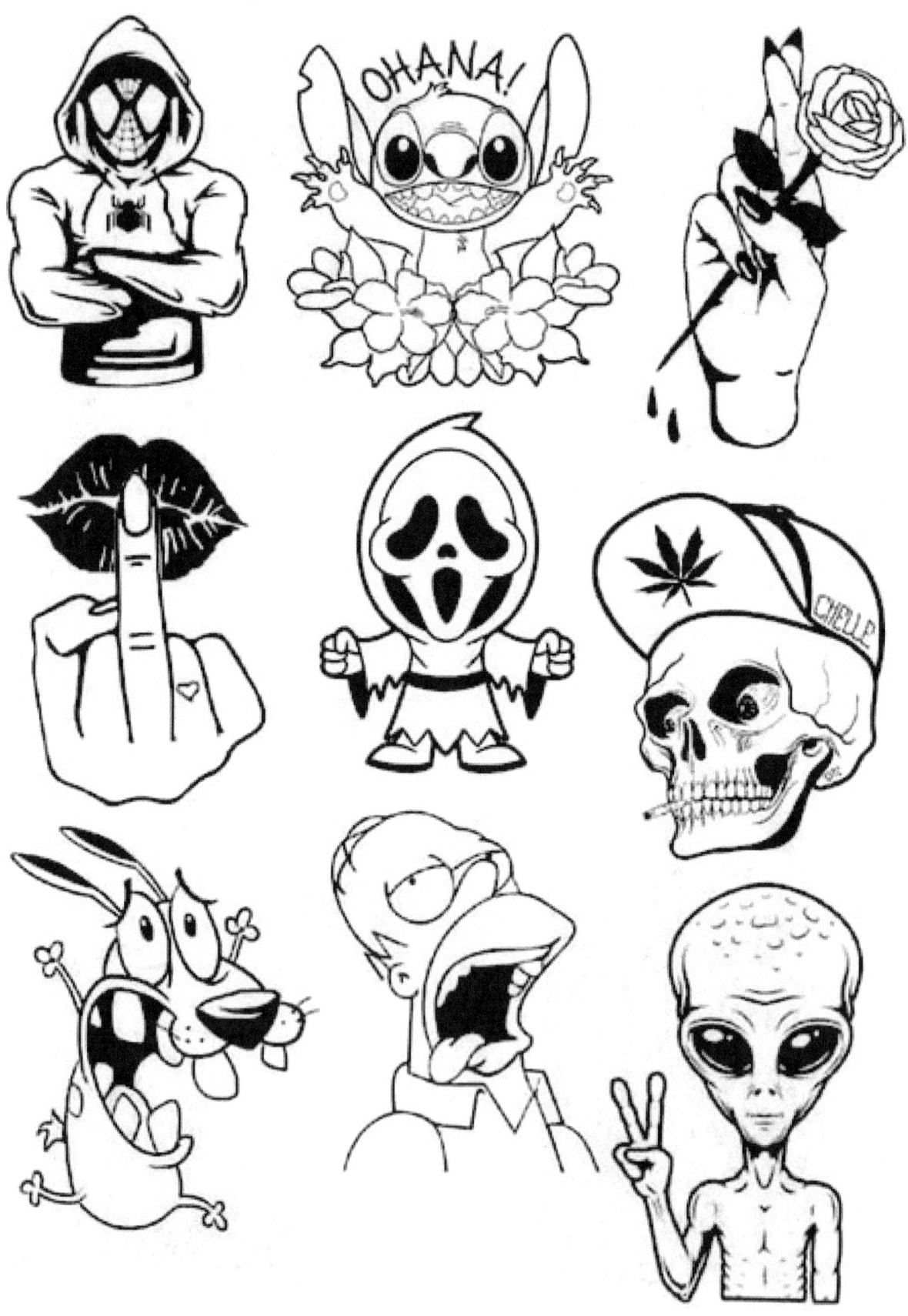

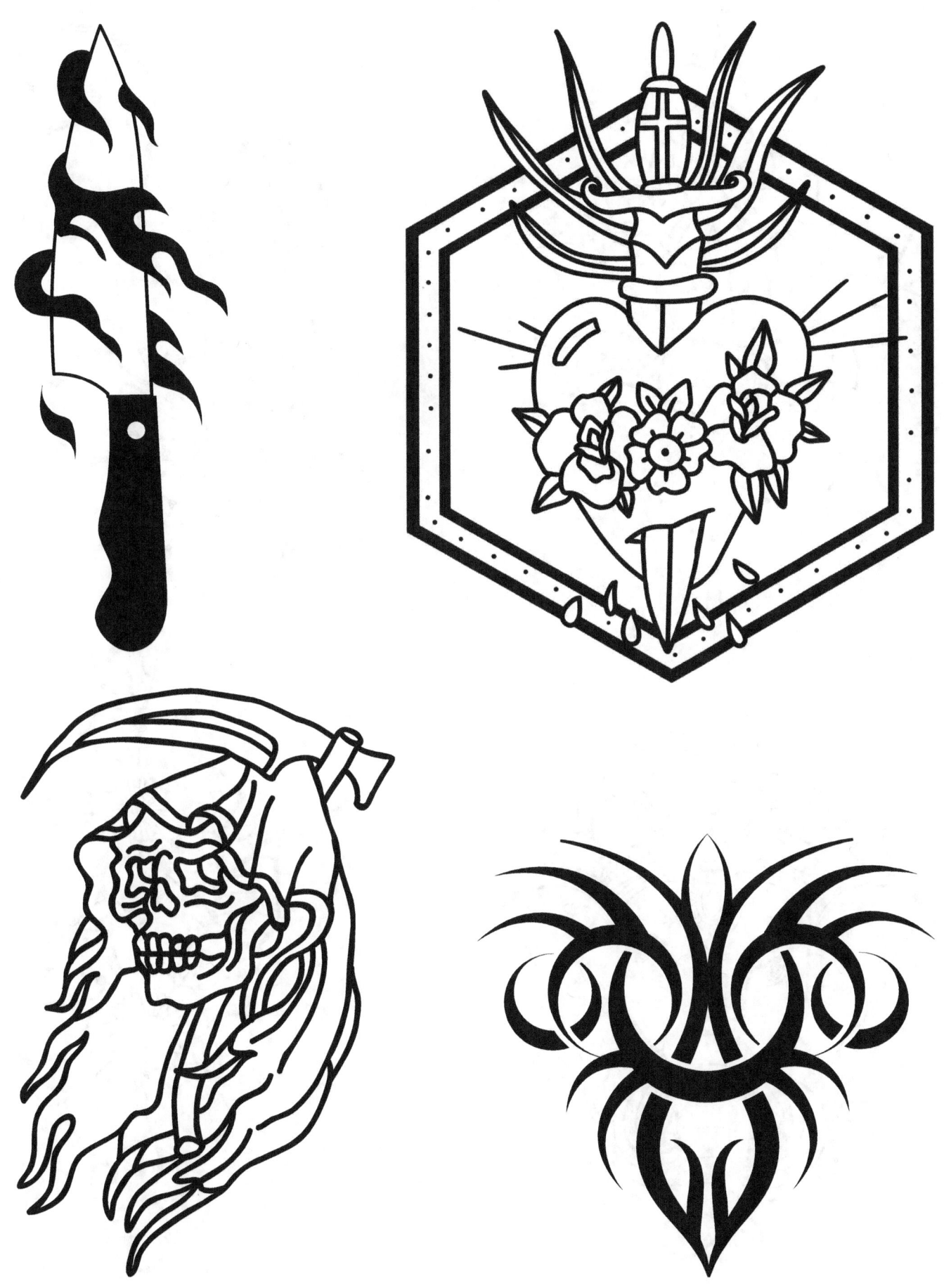

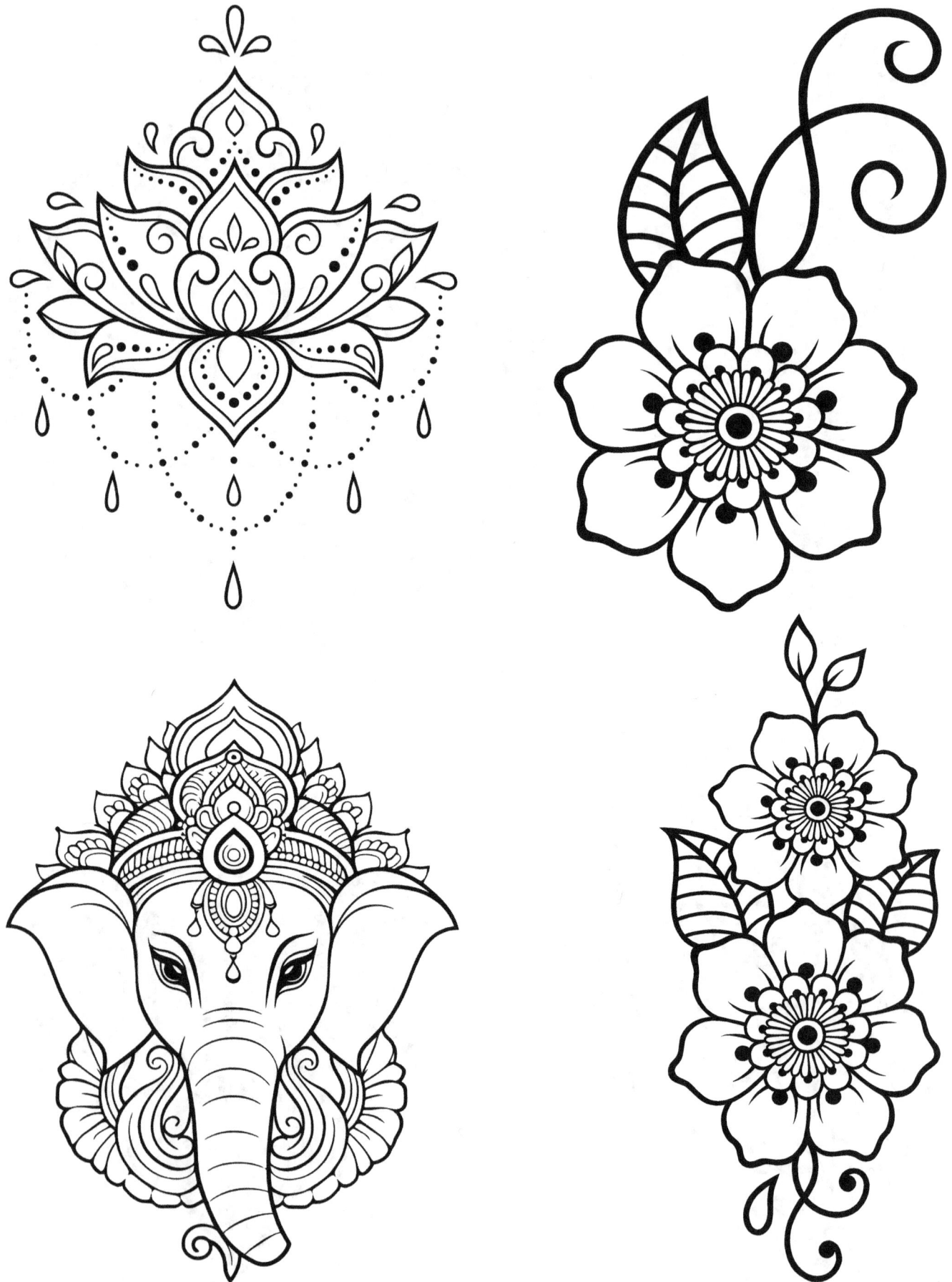

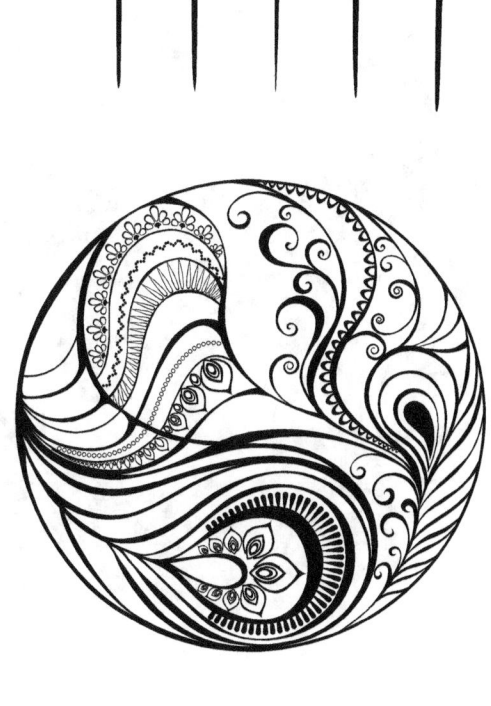

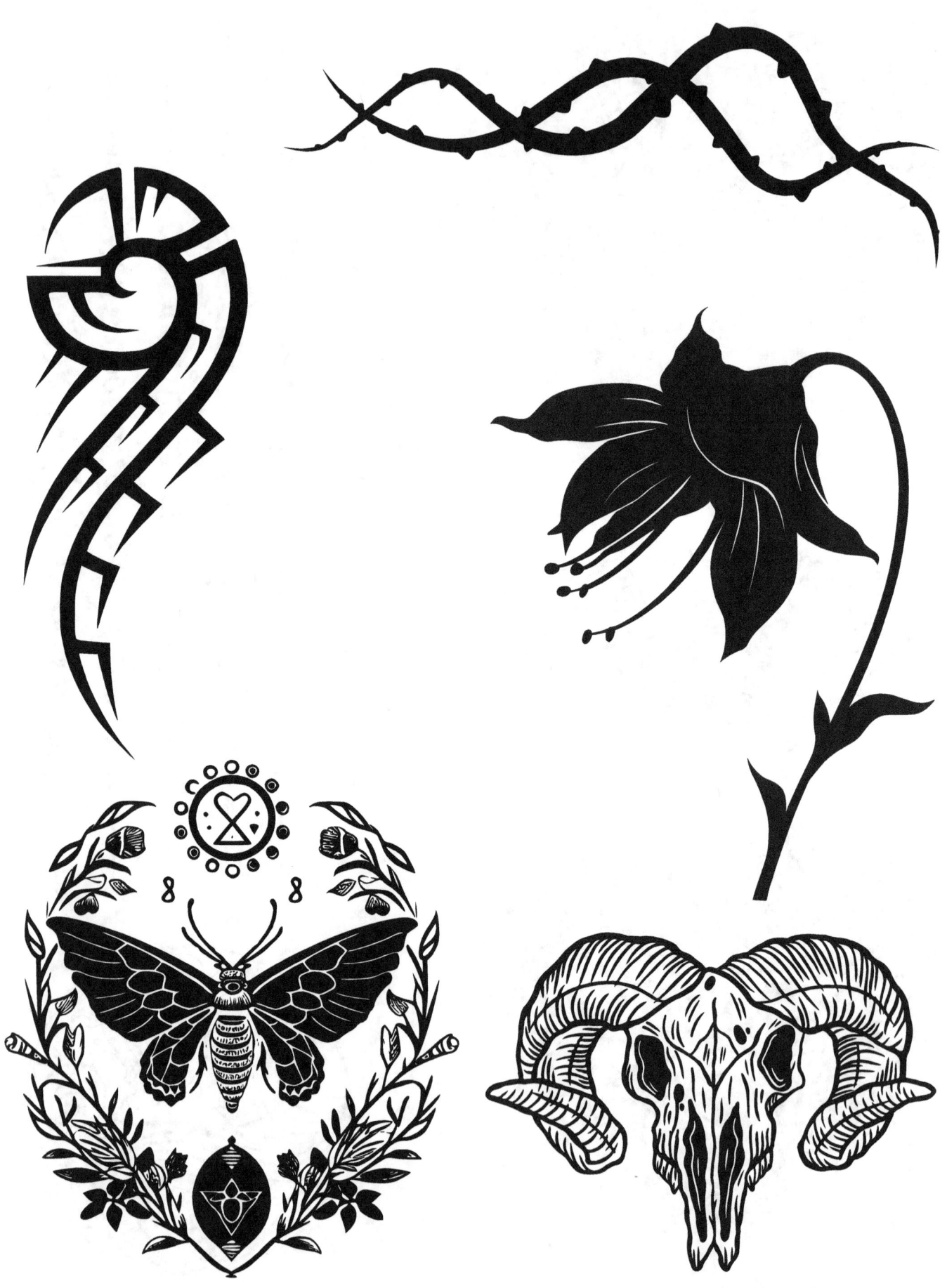

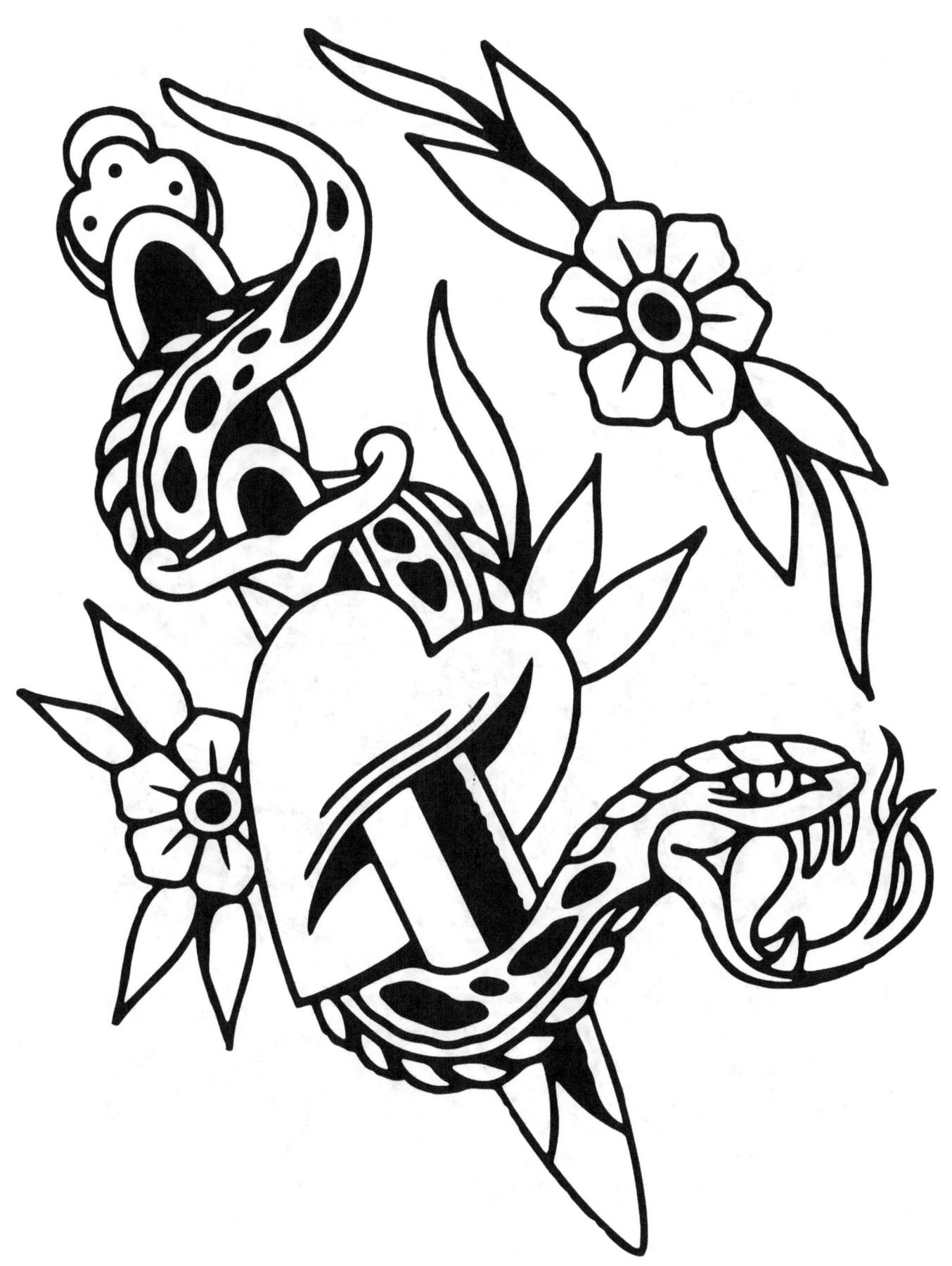

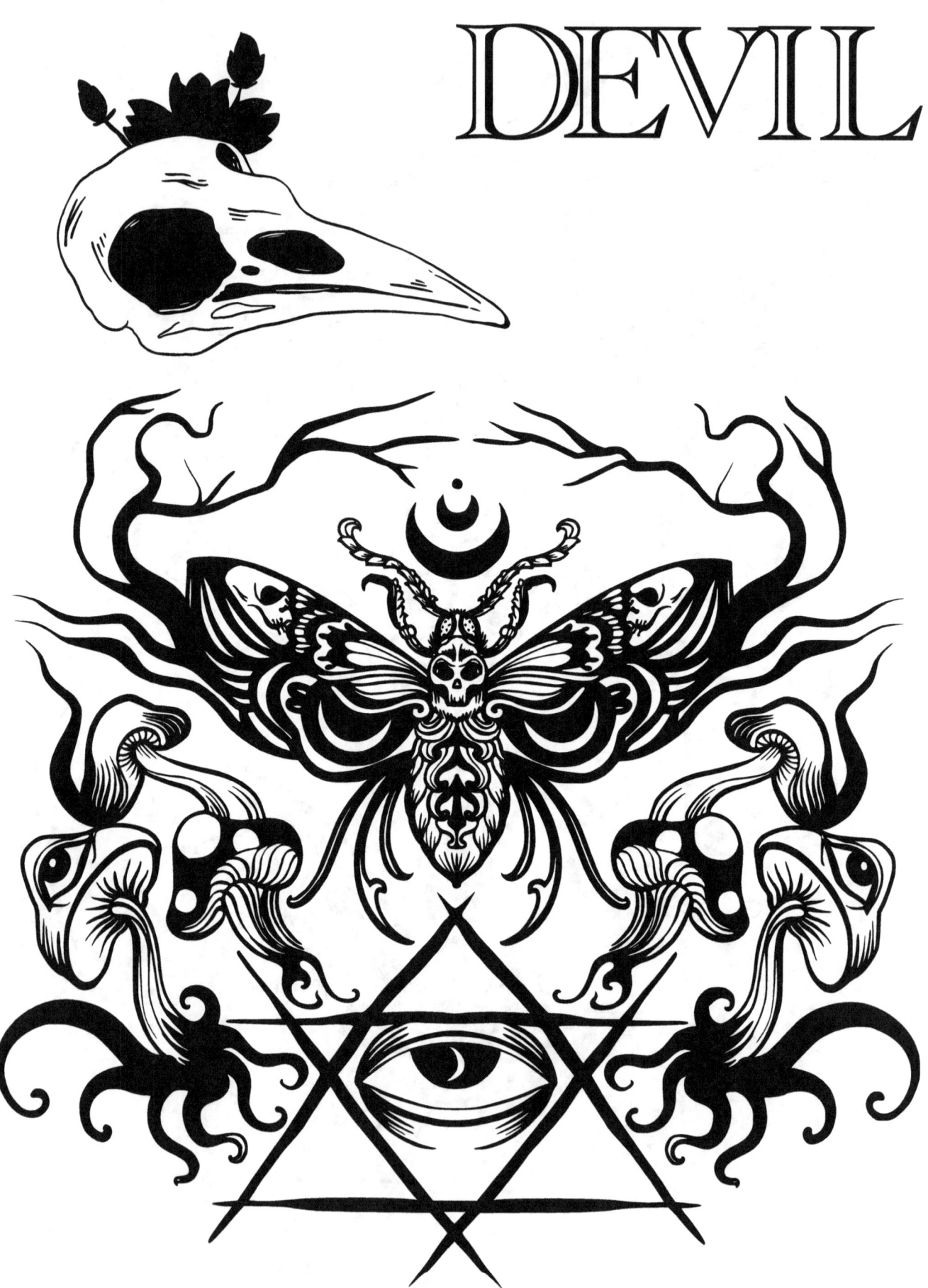

DEVIL

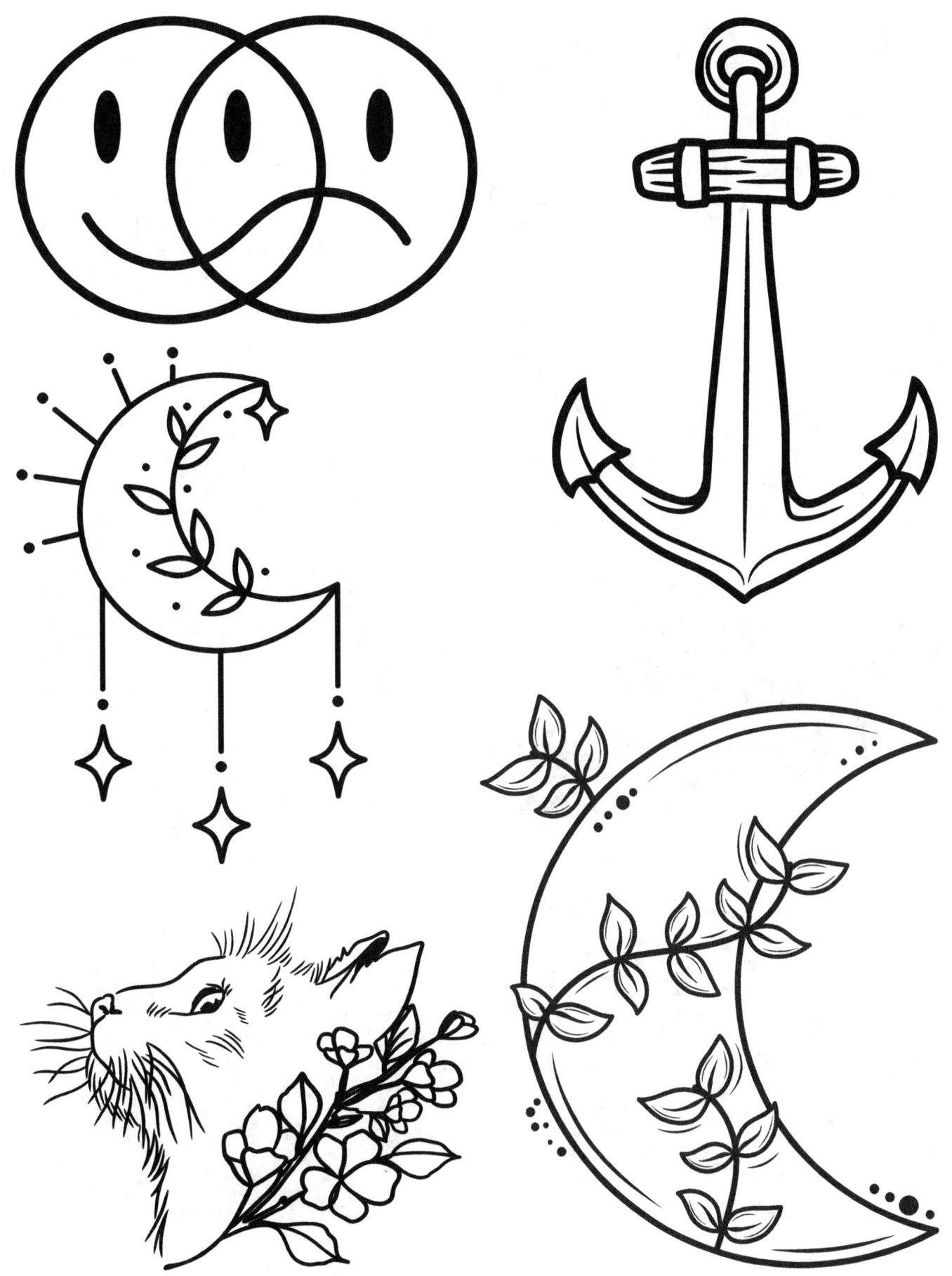

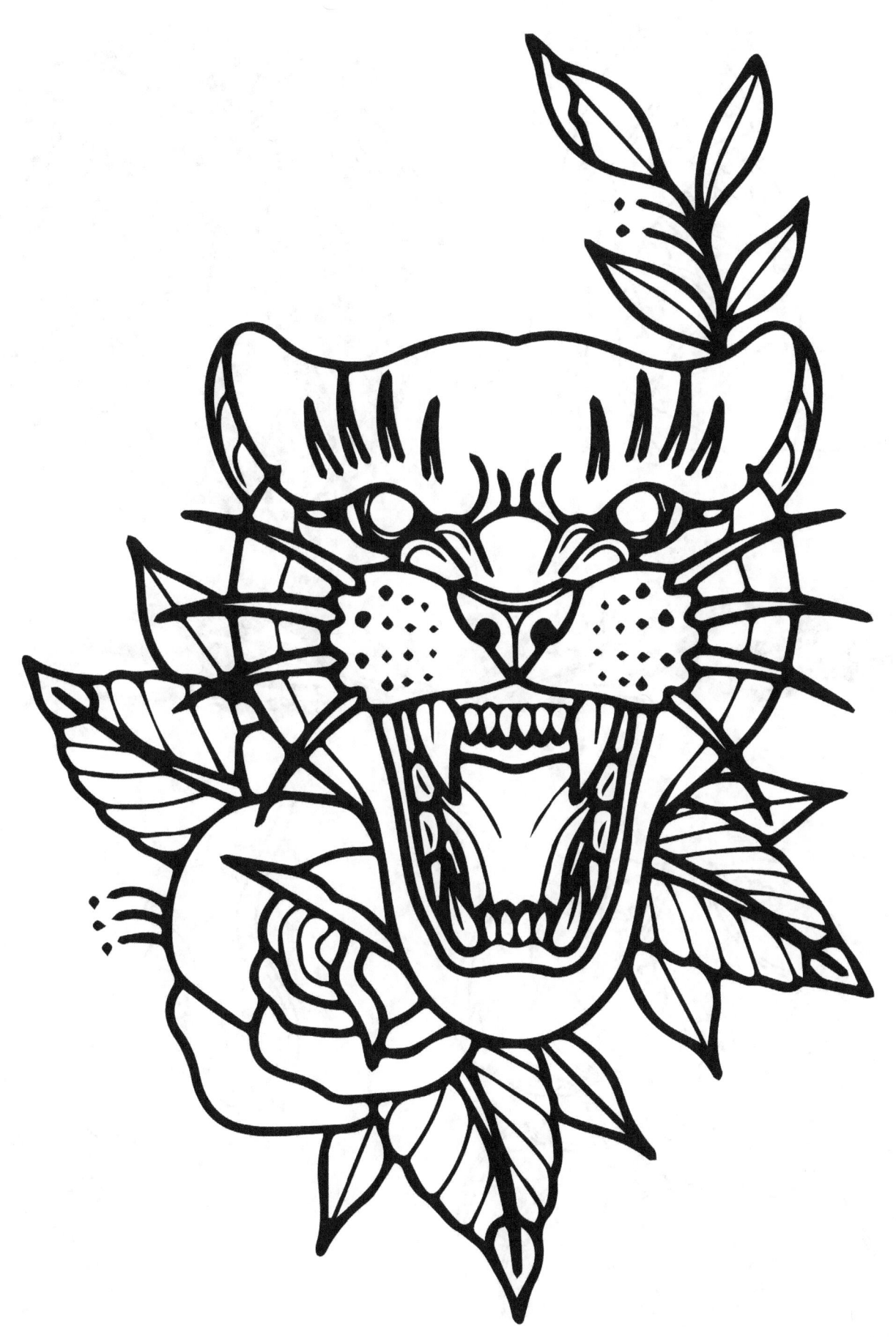

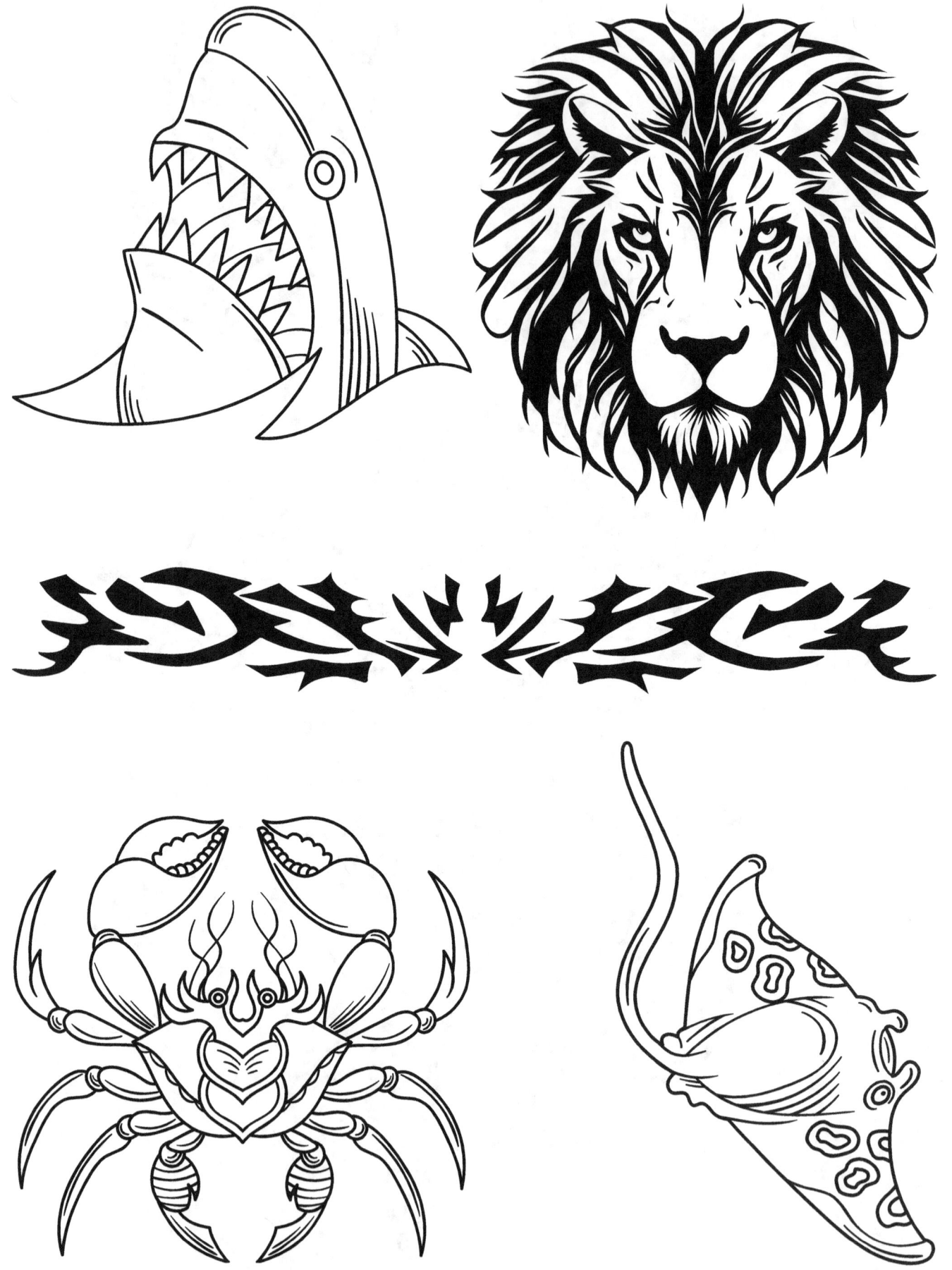

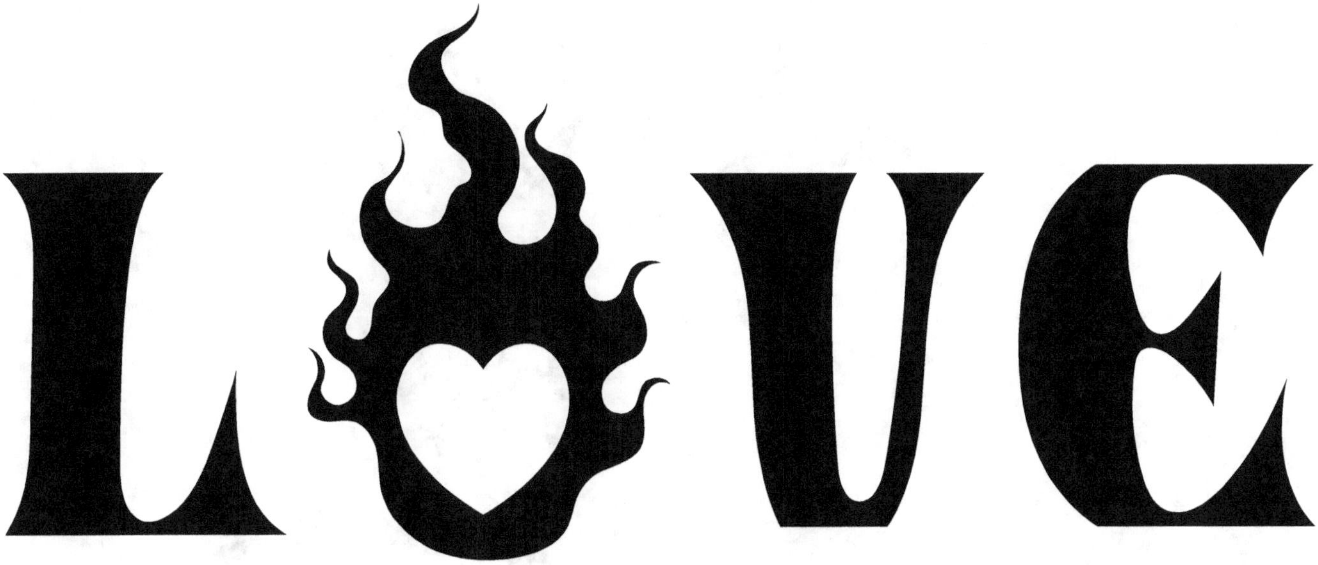
LOVE

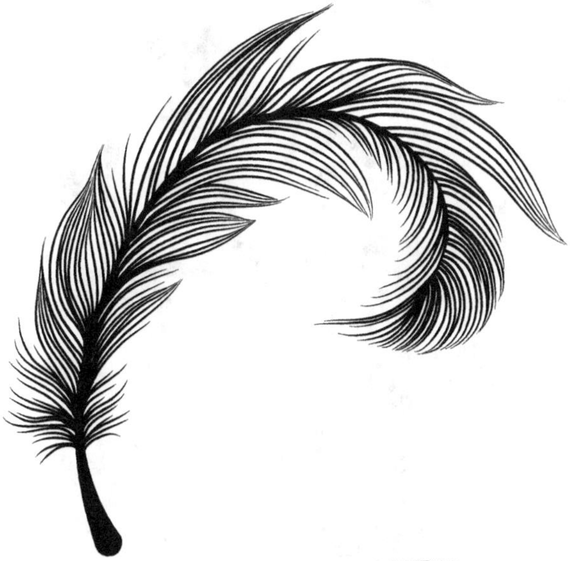

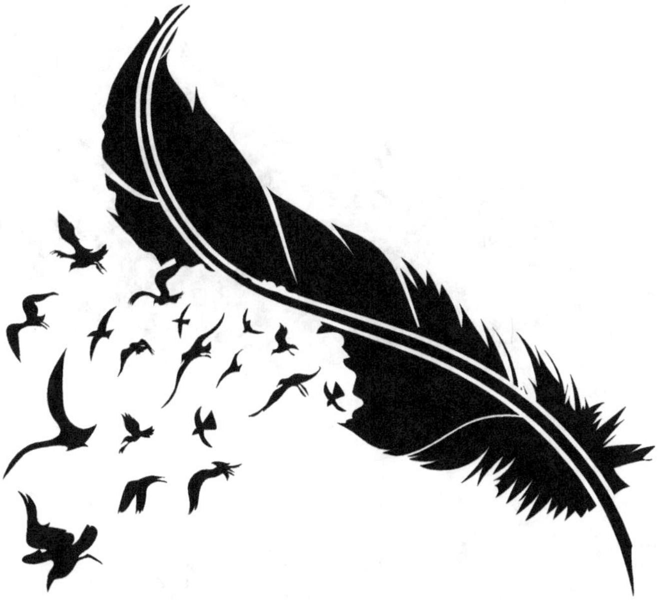

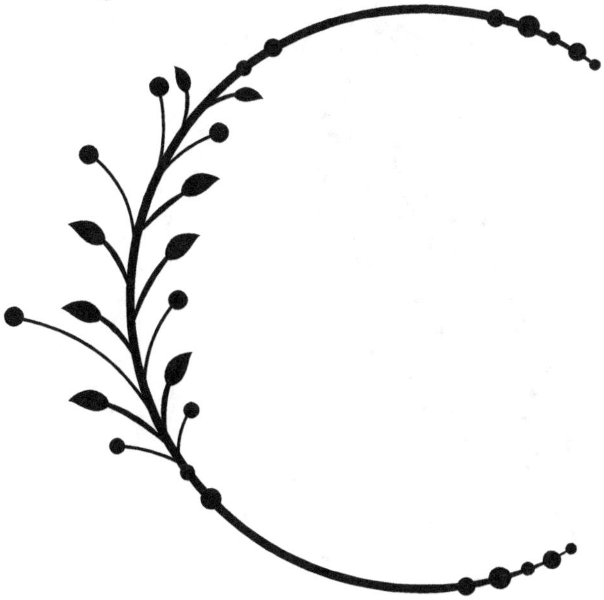

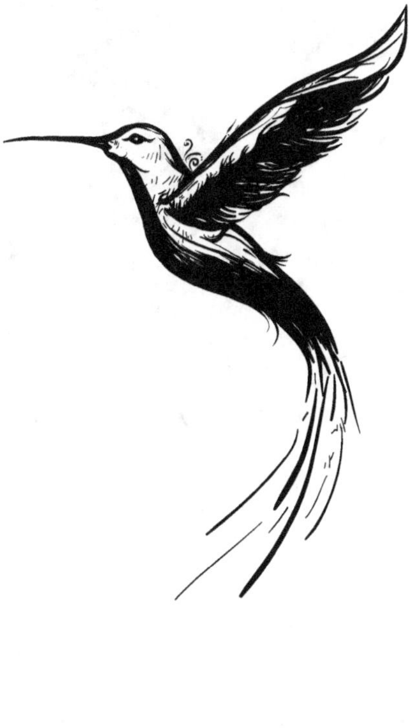

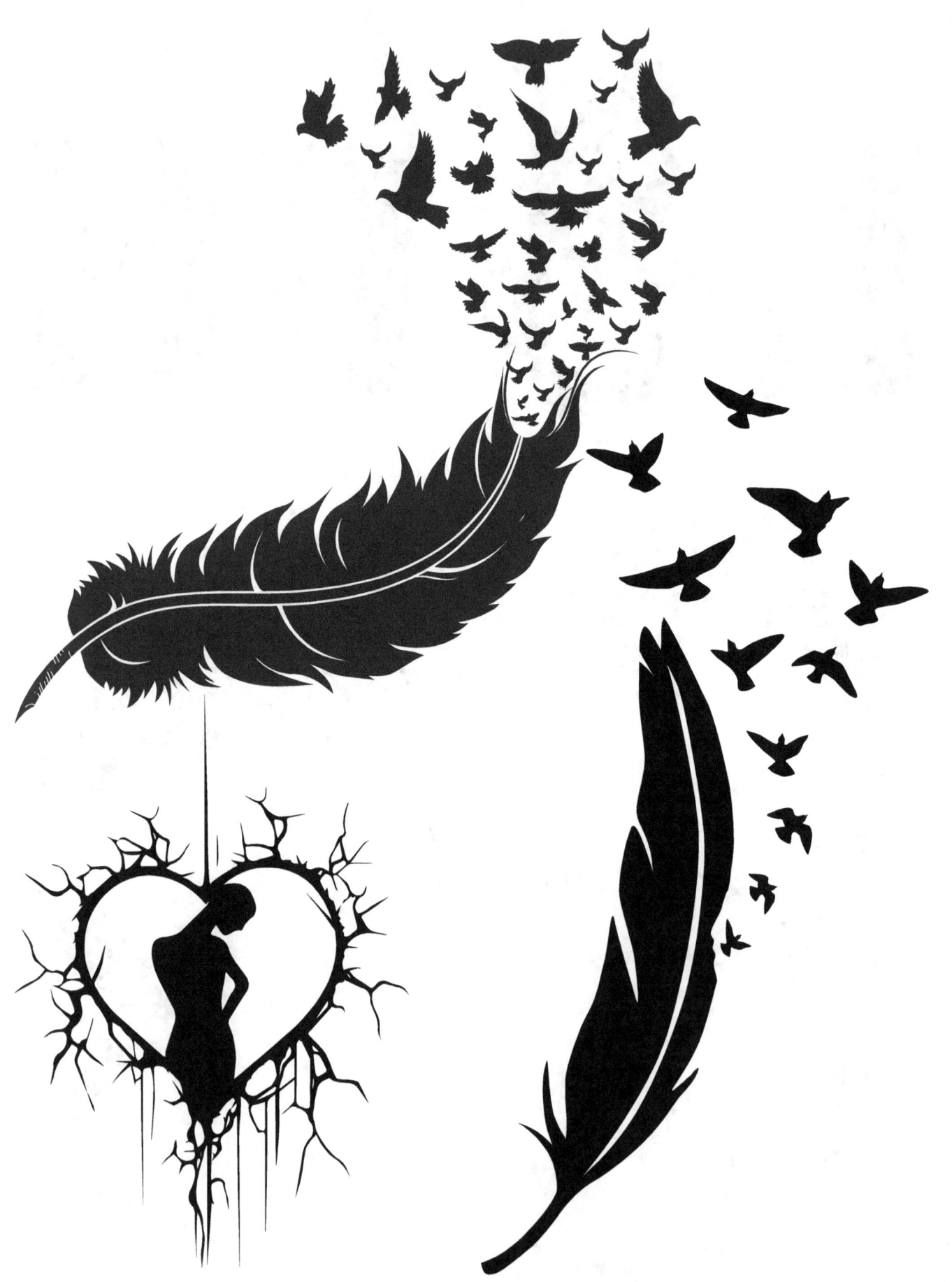

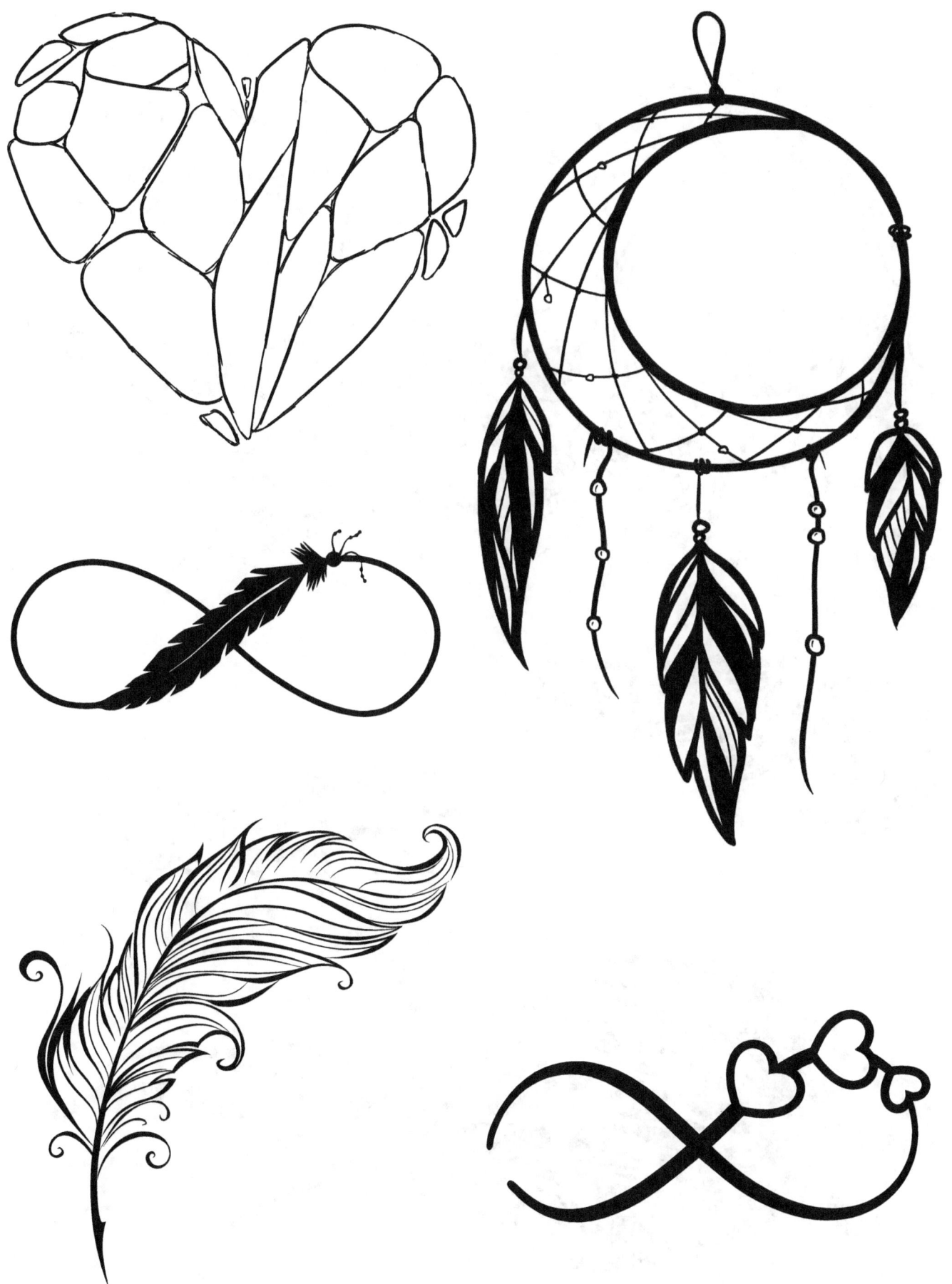

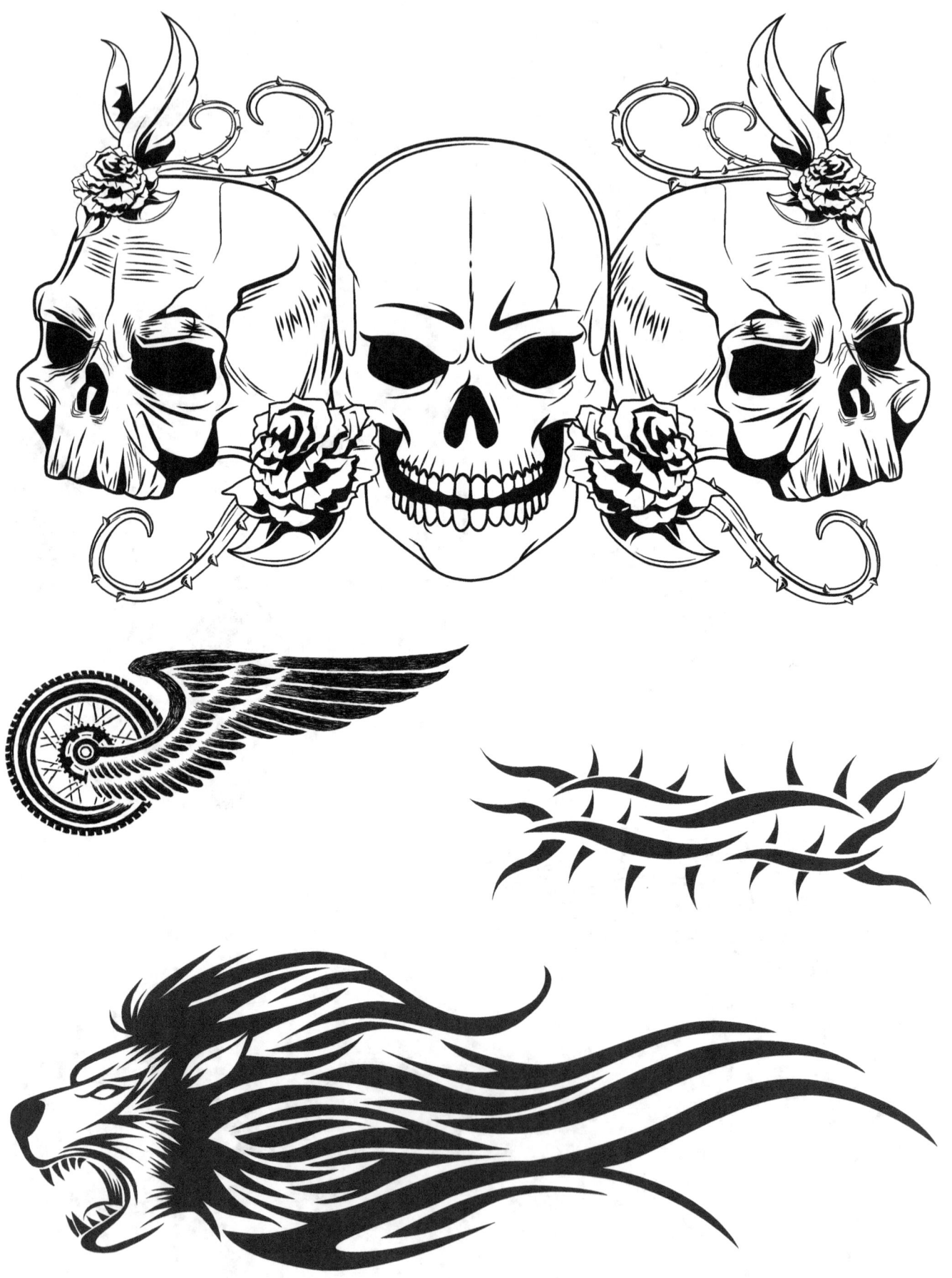

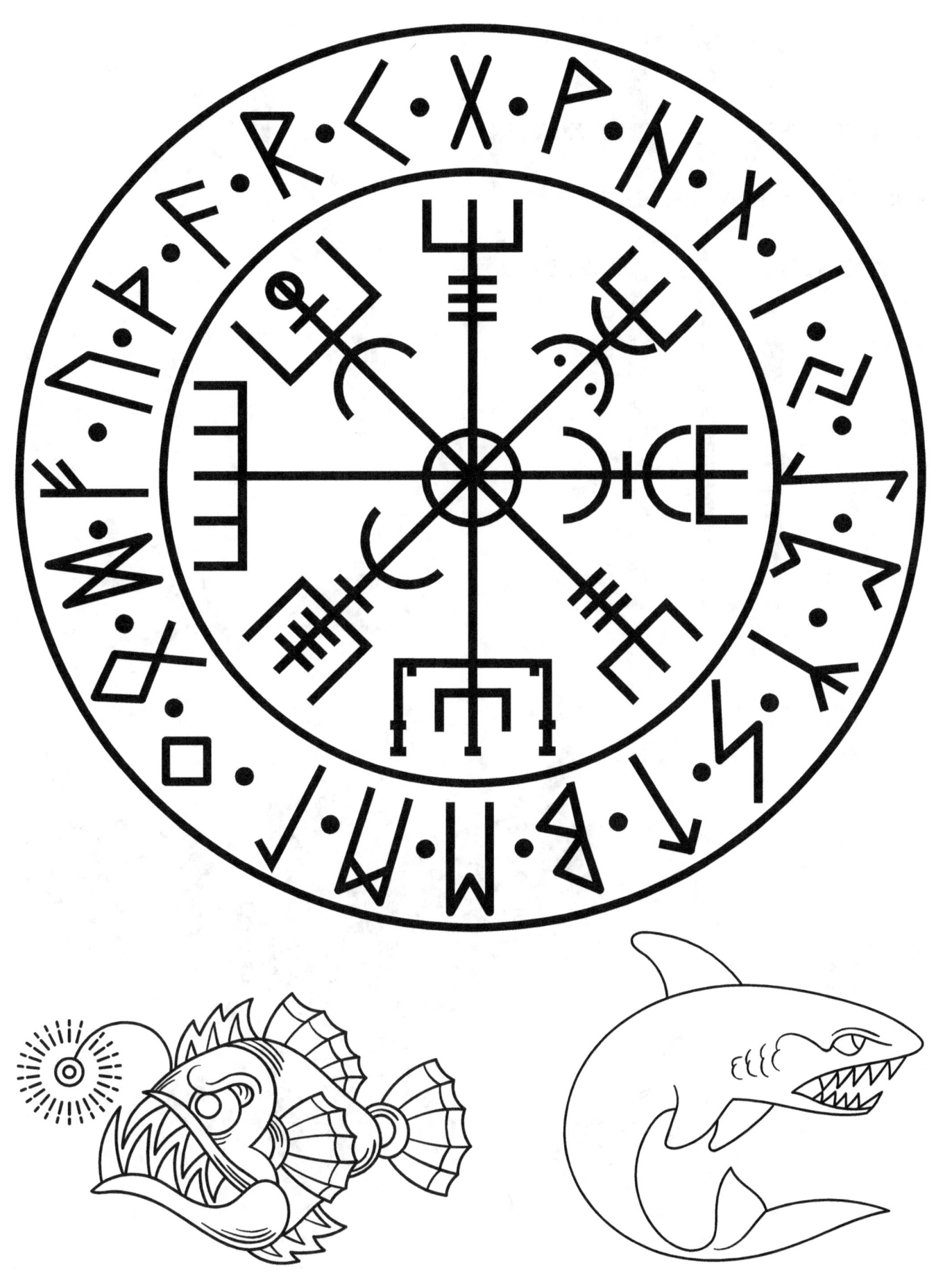

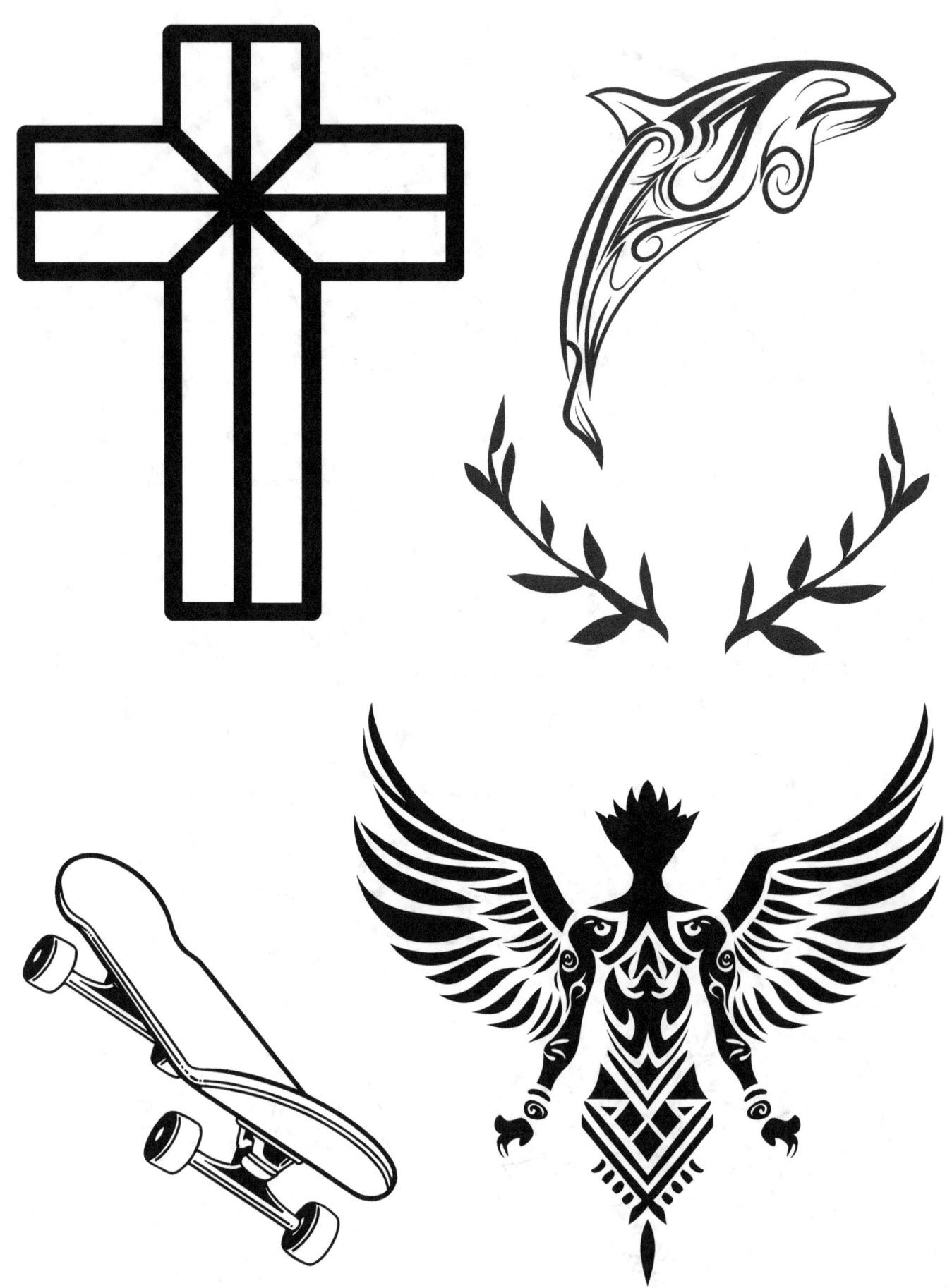

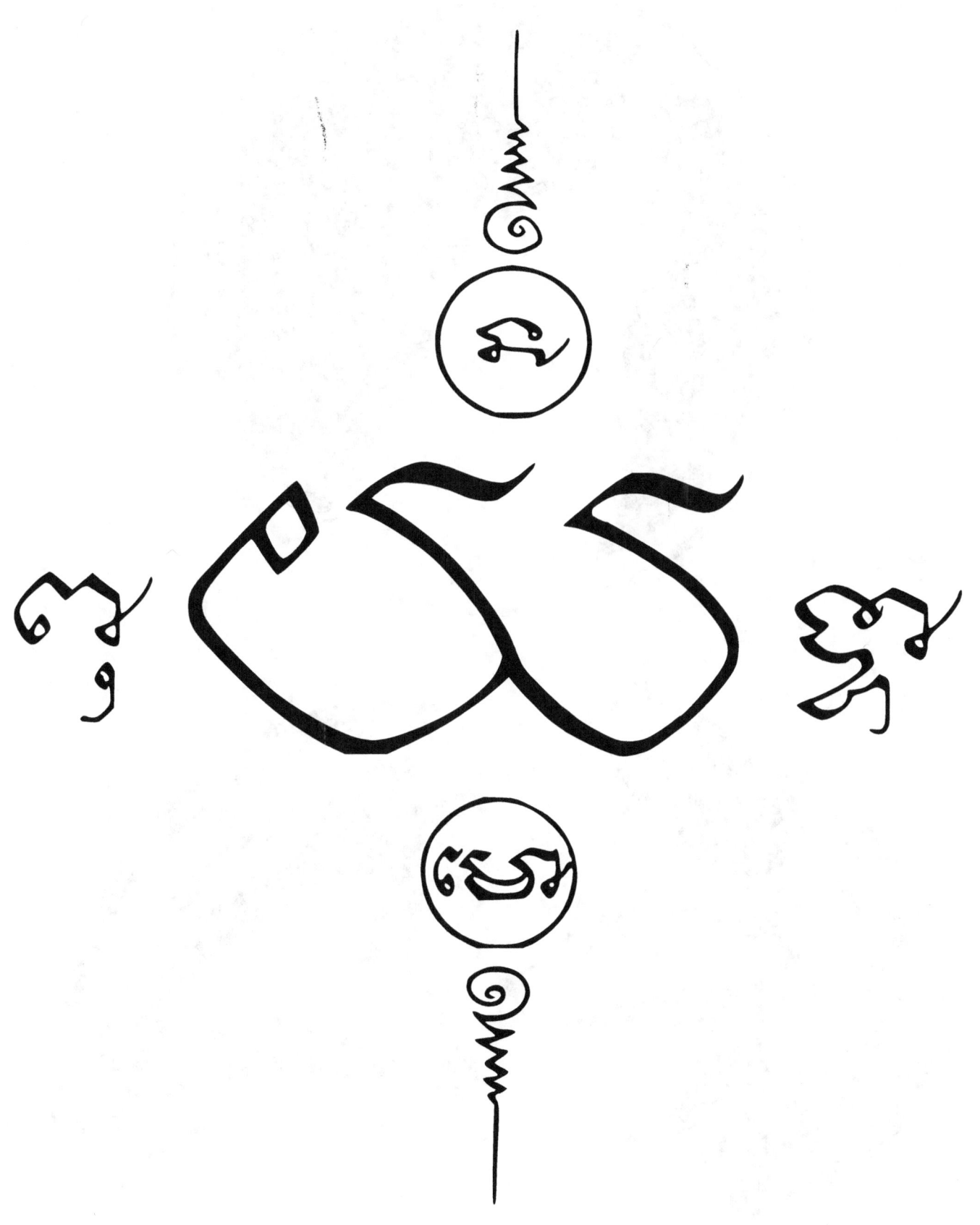

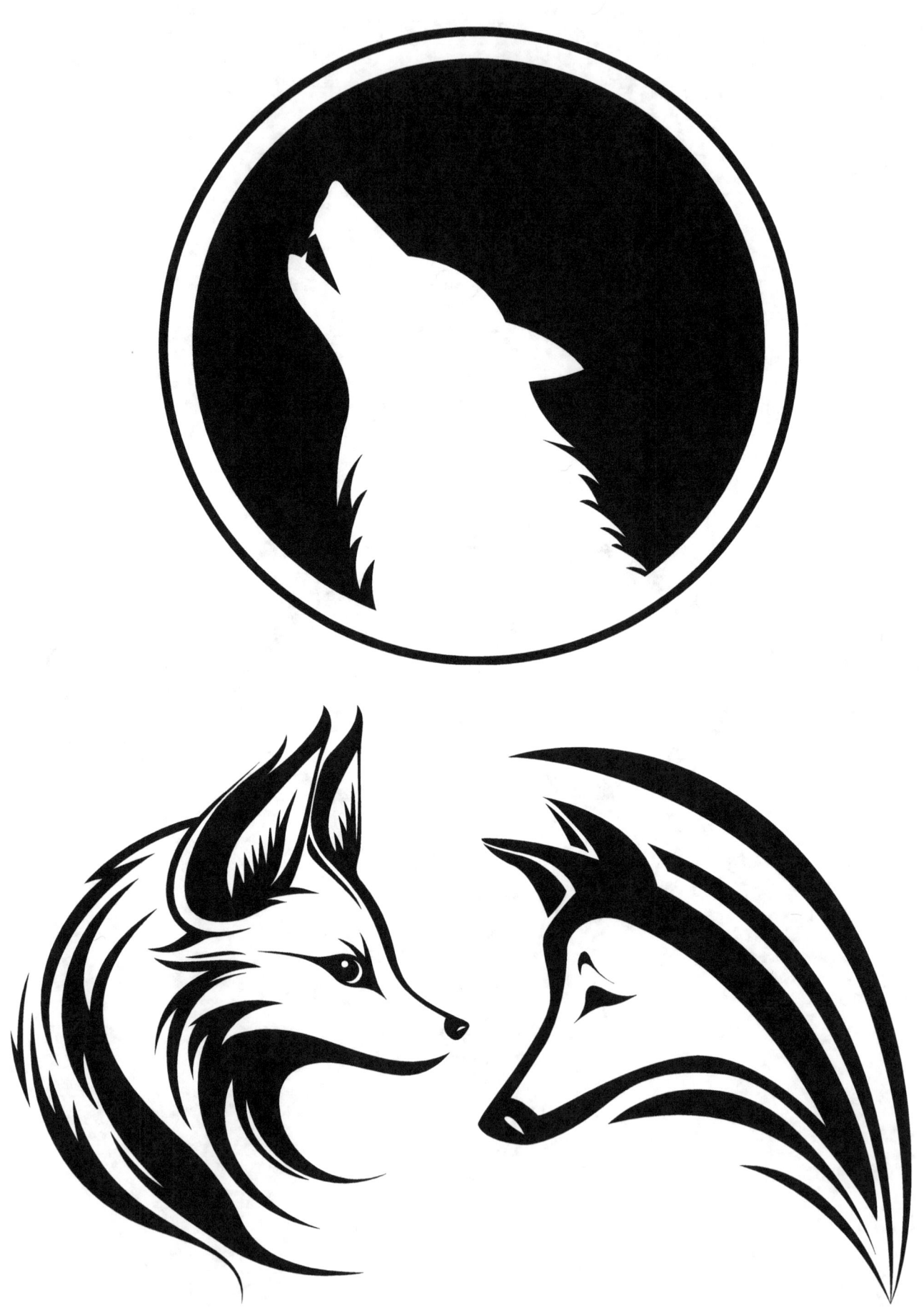

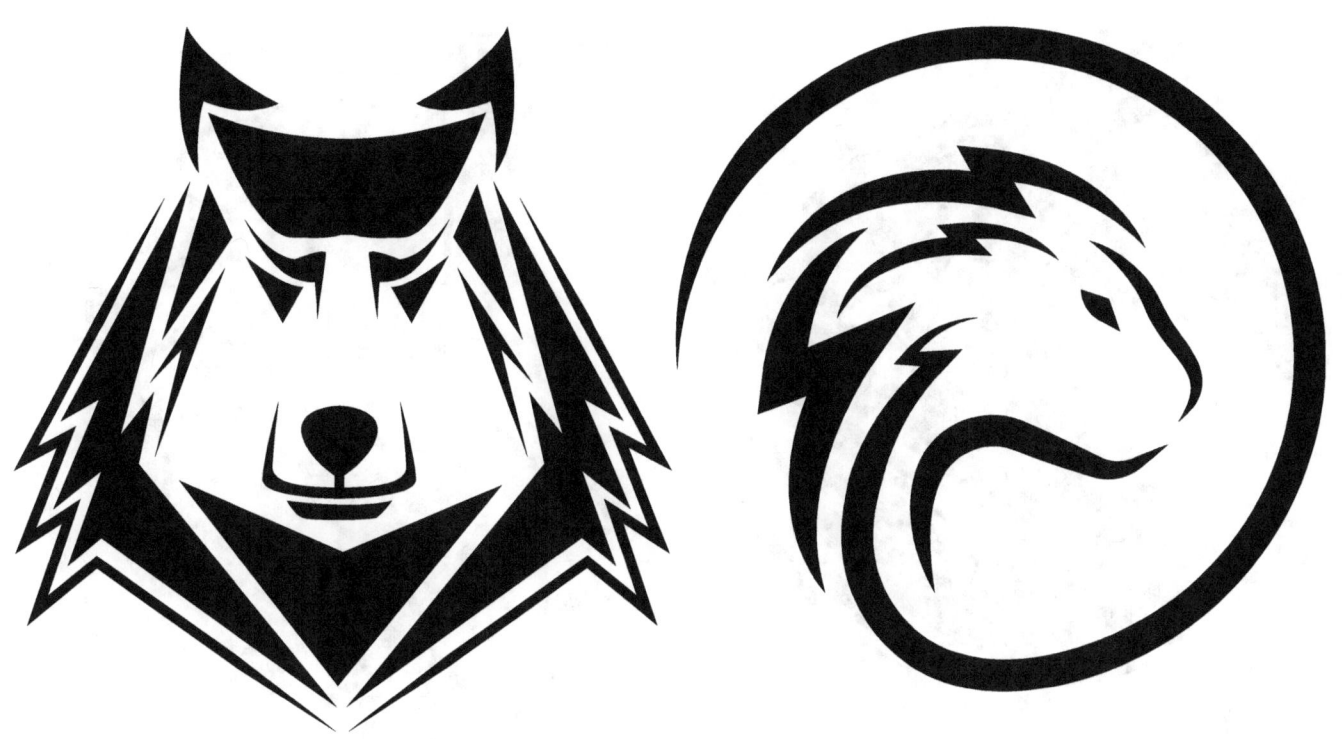
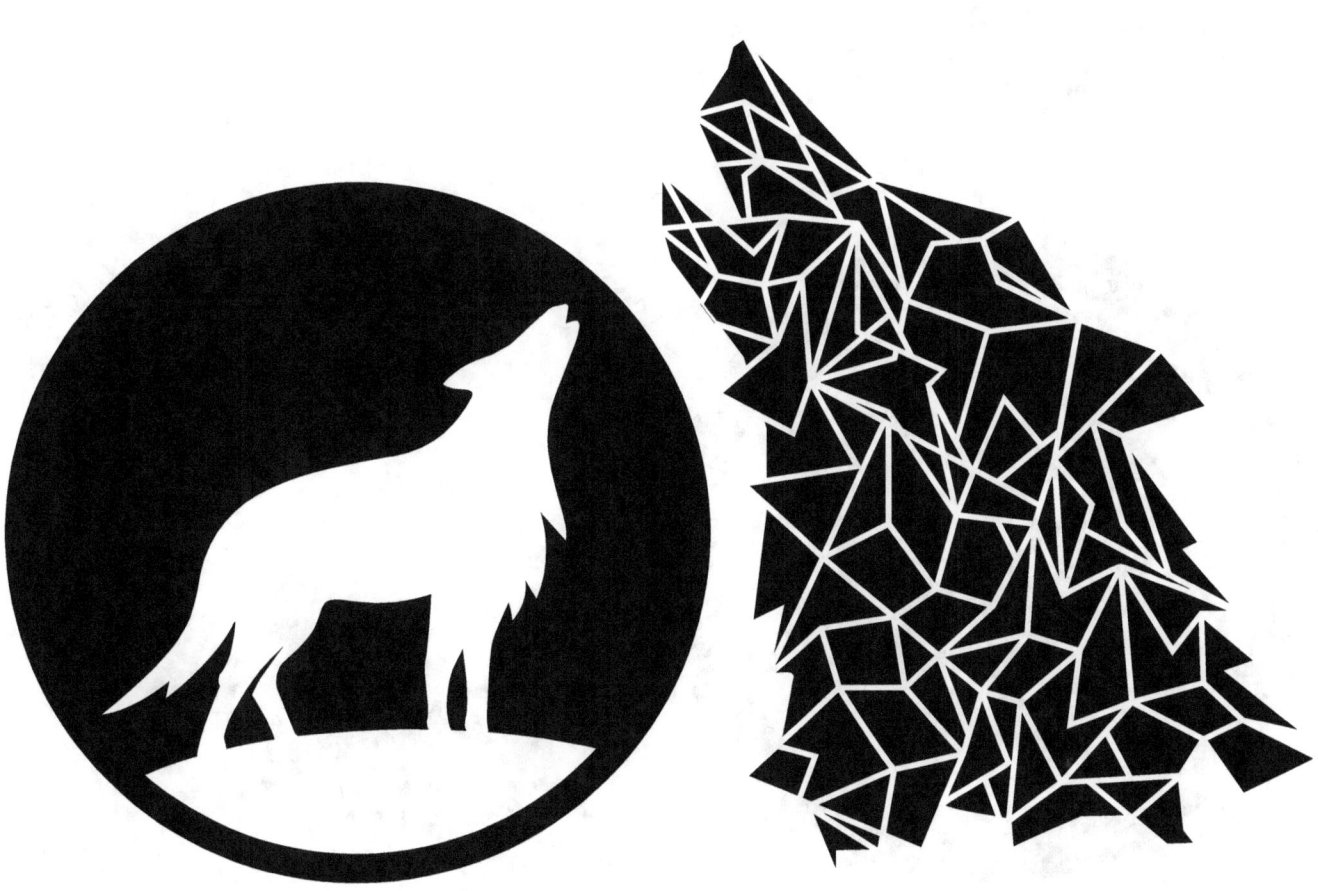

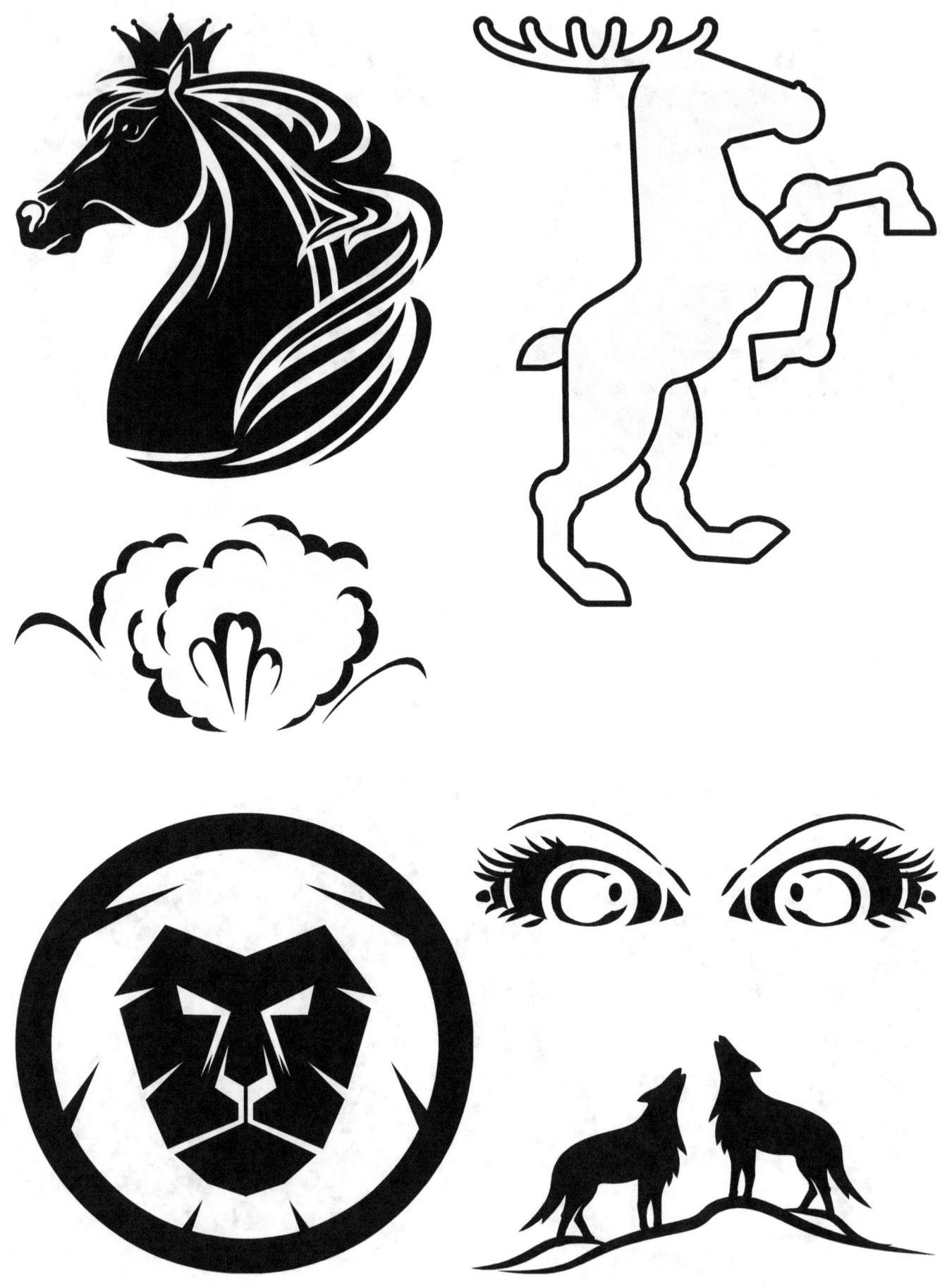

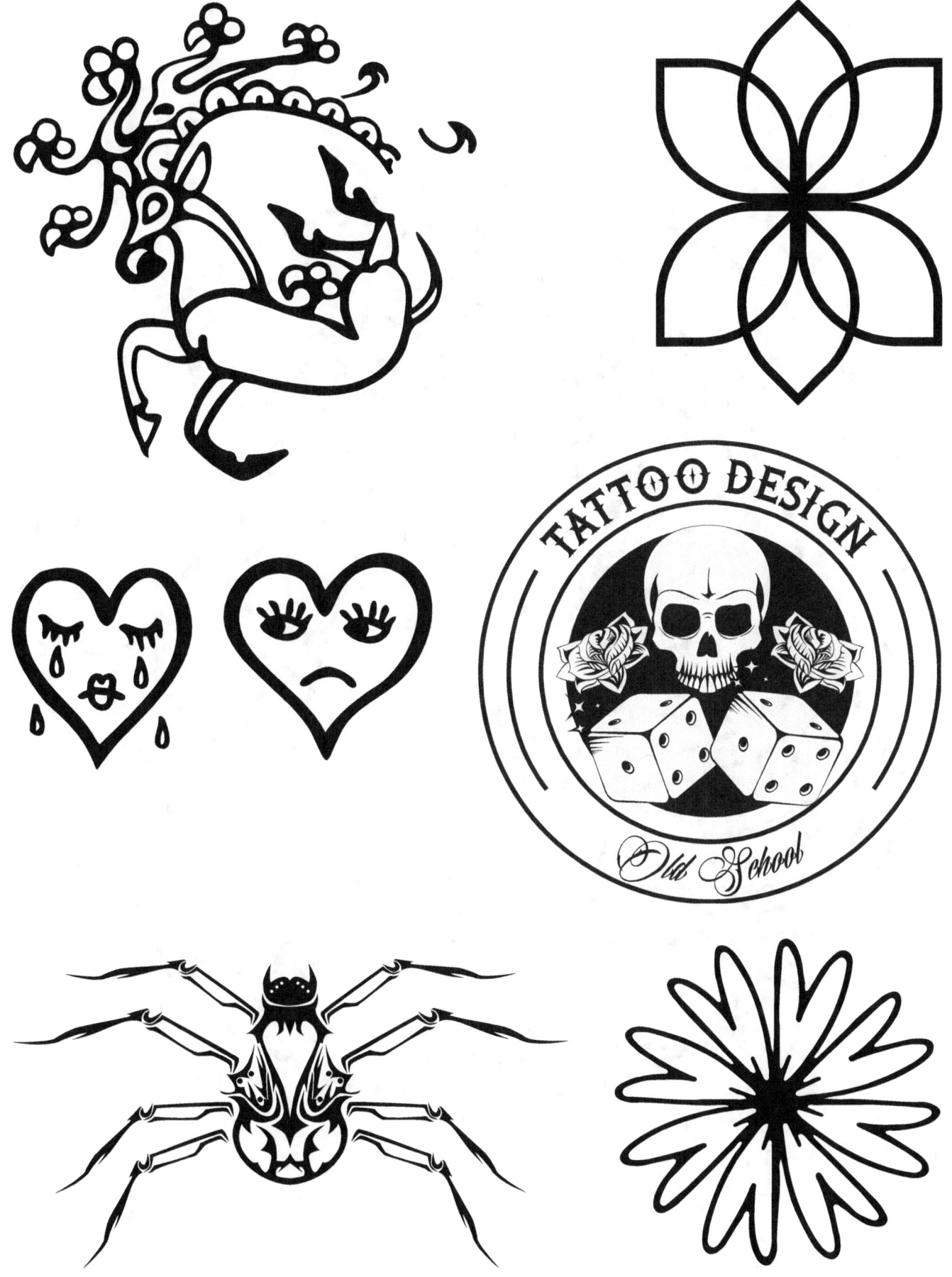

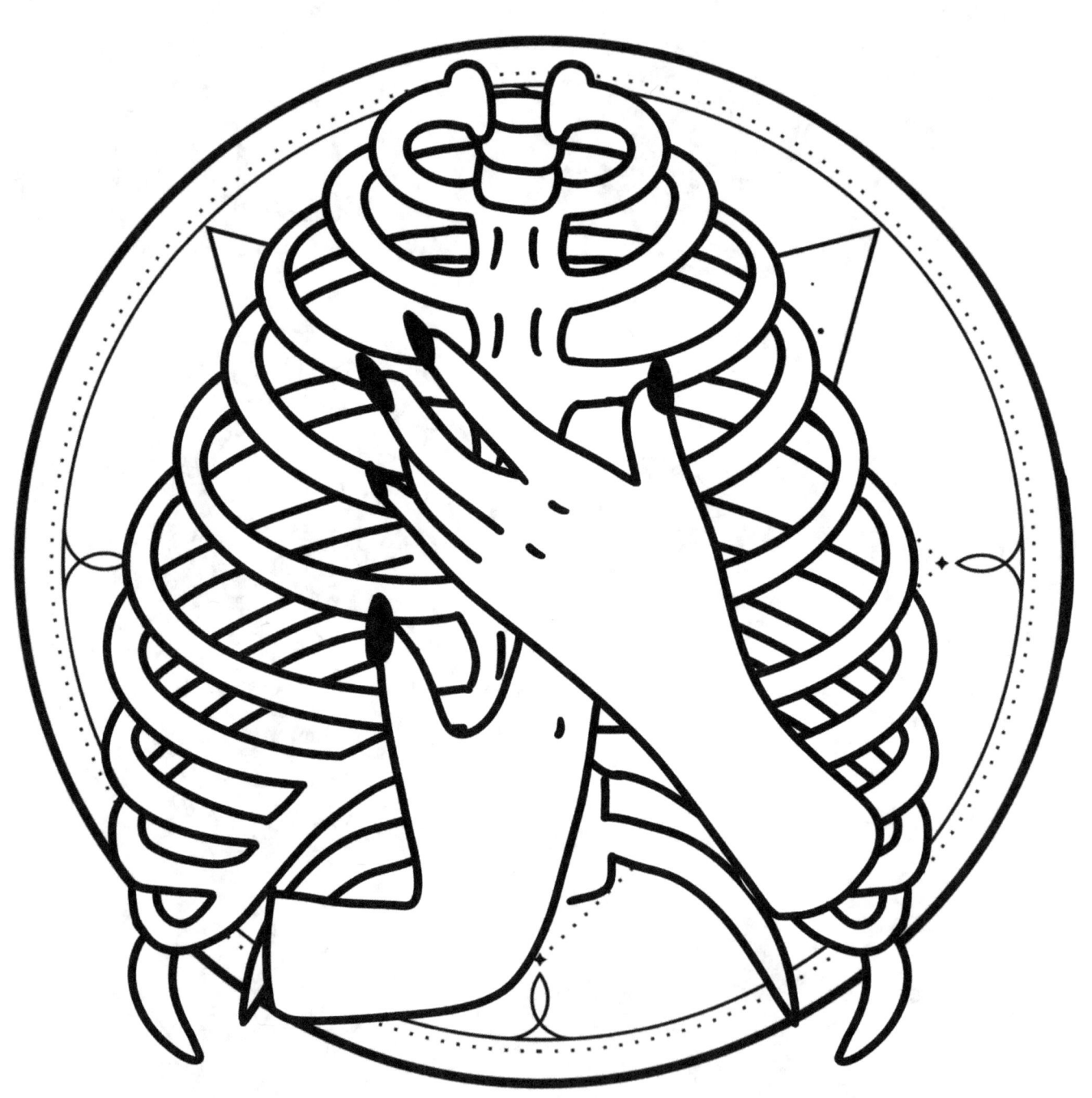

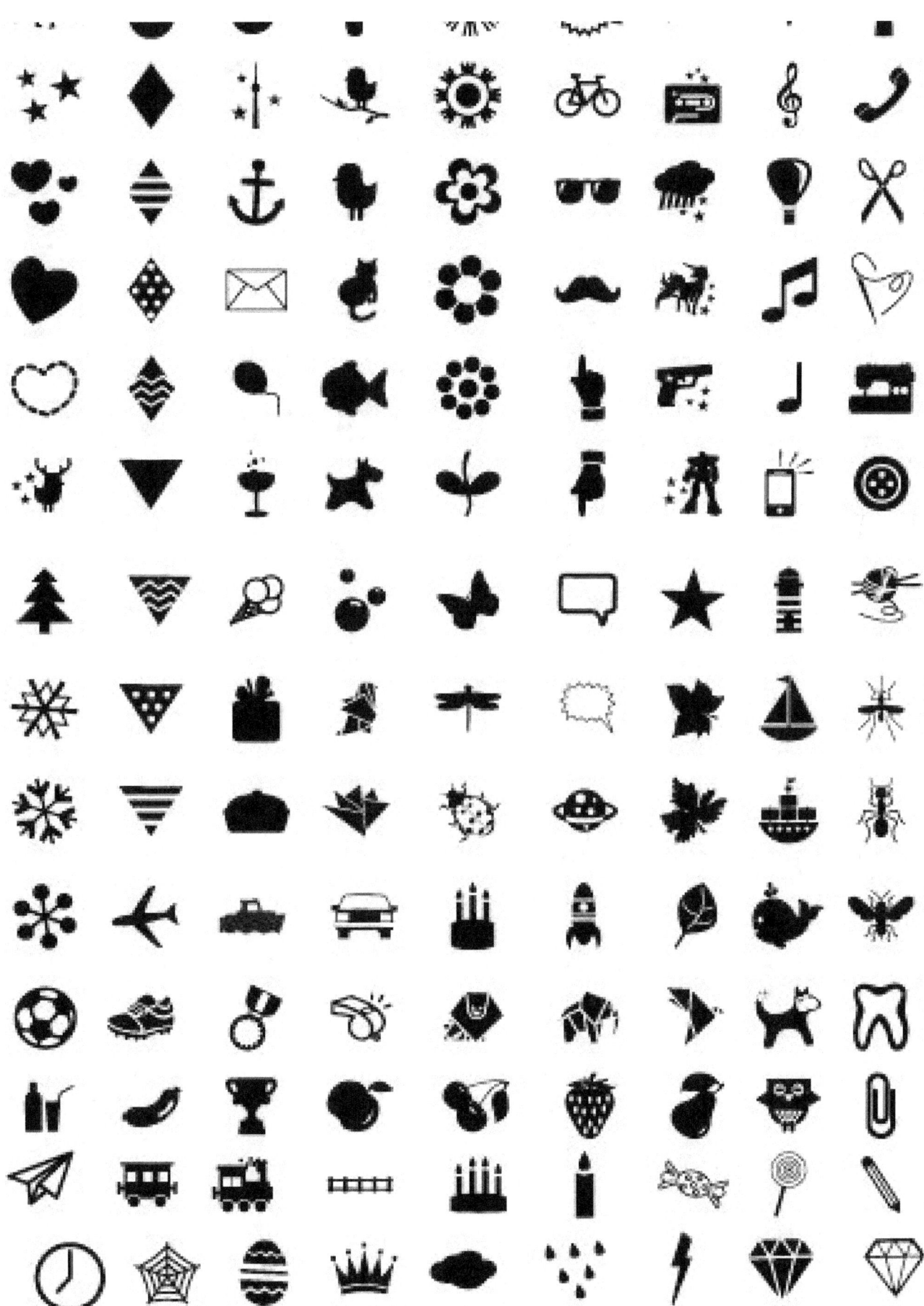

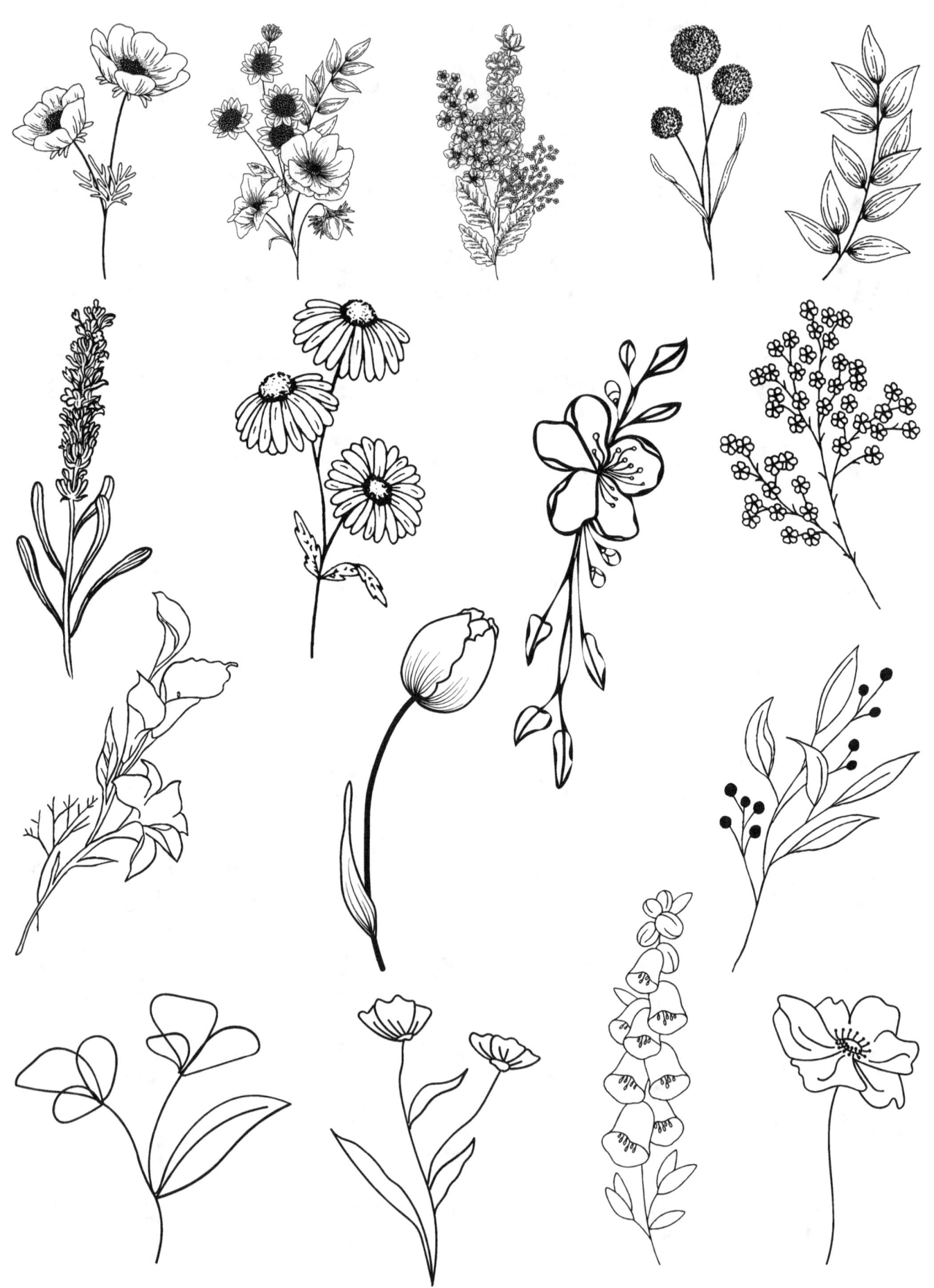

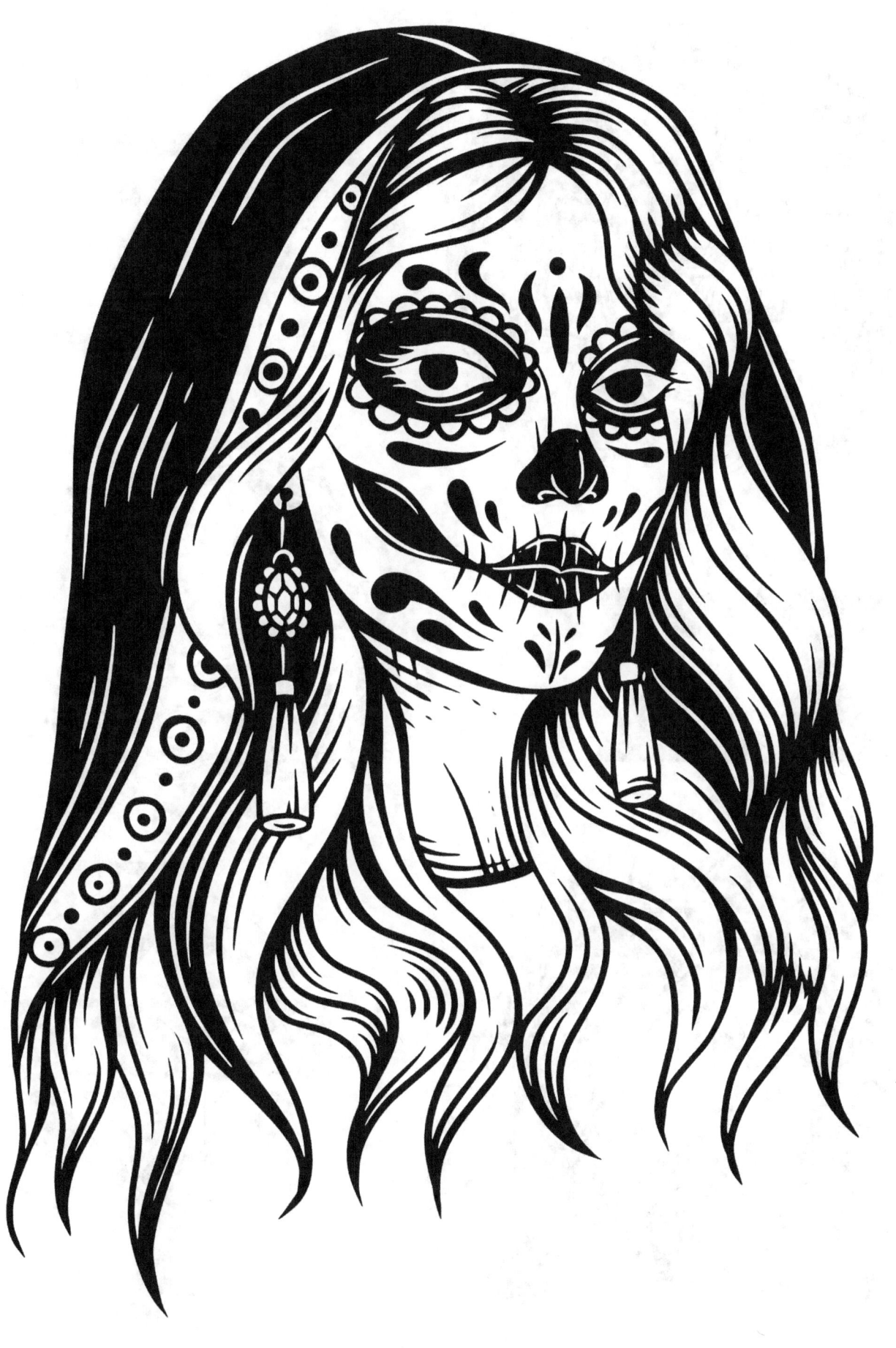

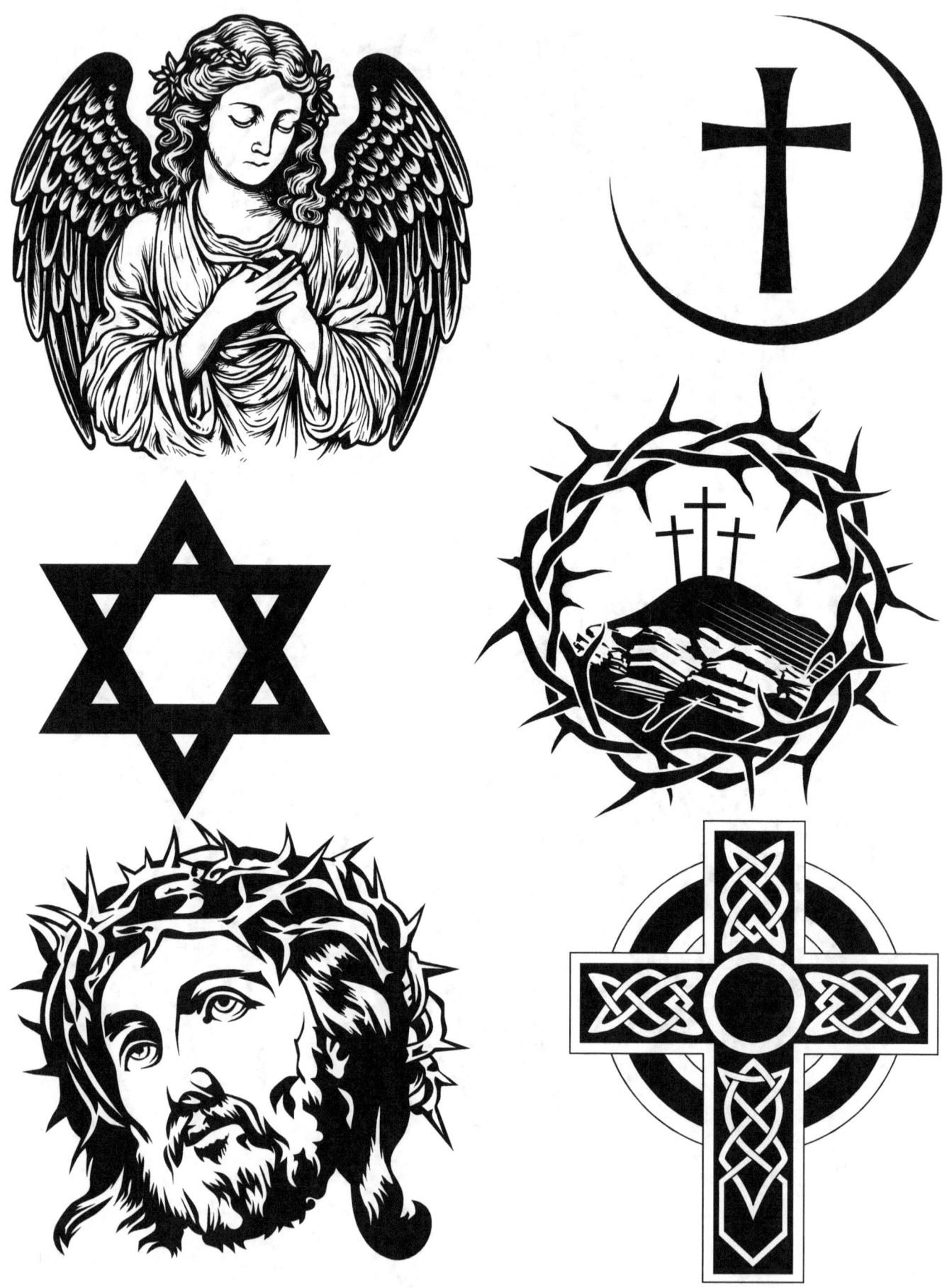

A B C D E F

G H I J K L

M N Ñ O P

Q R S T U

V W X Y Z

abcdef
ghijkl
mnñop
qrstuv
wxyz

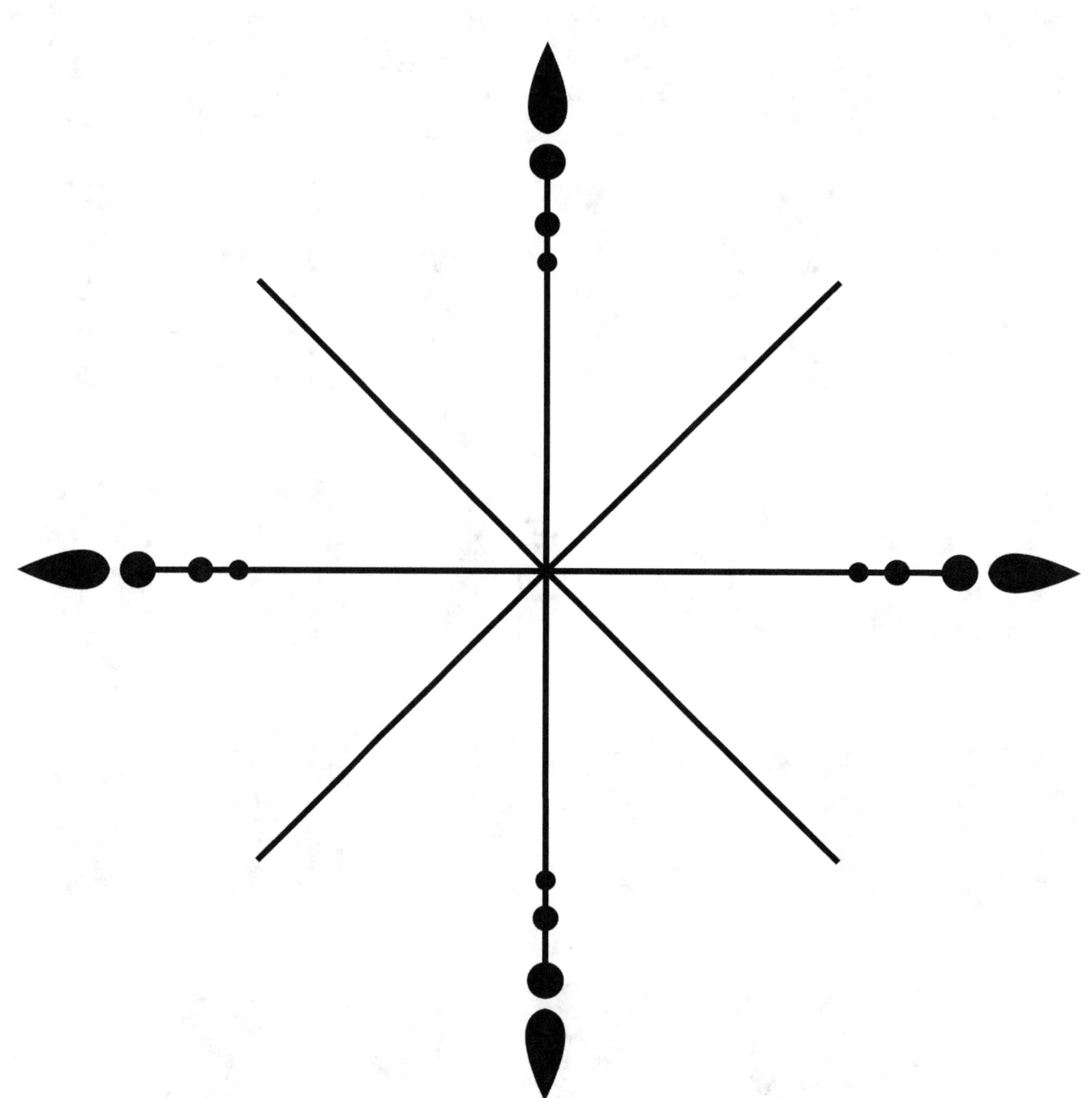

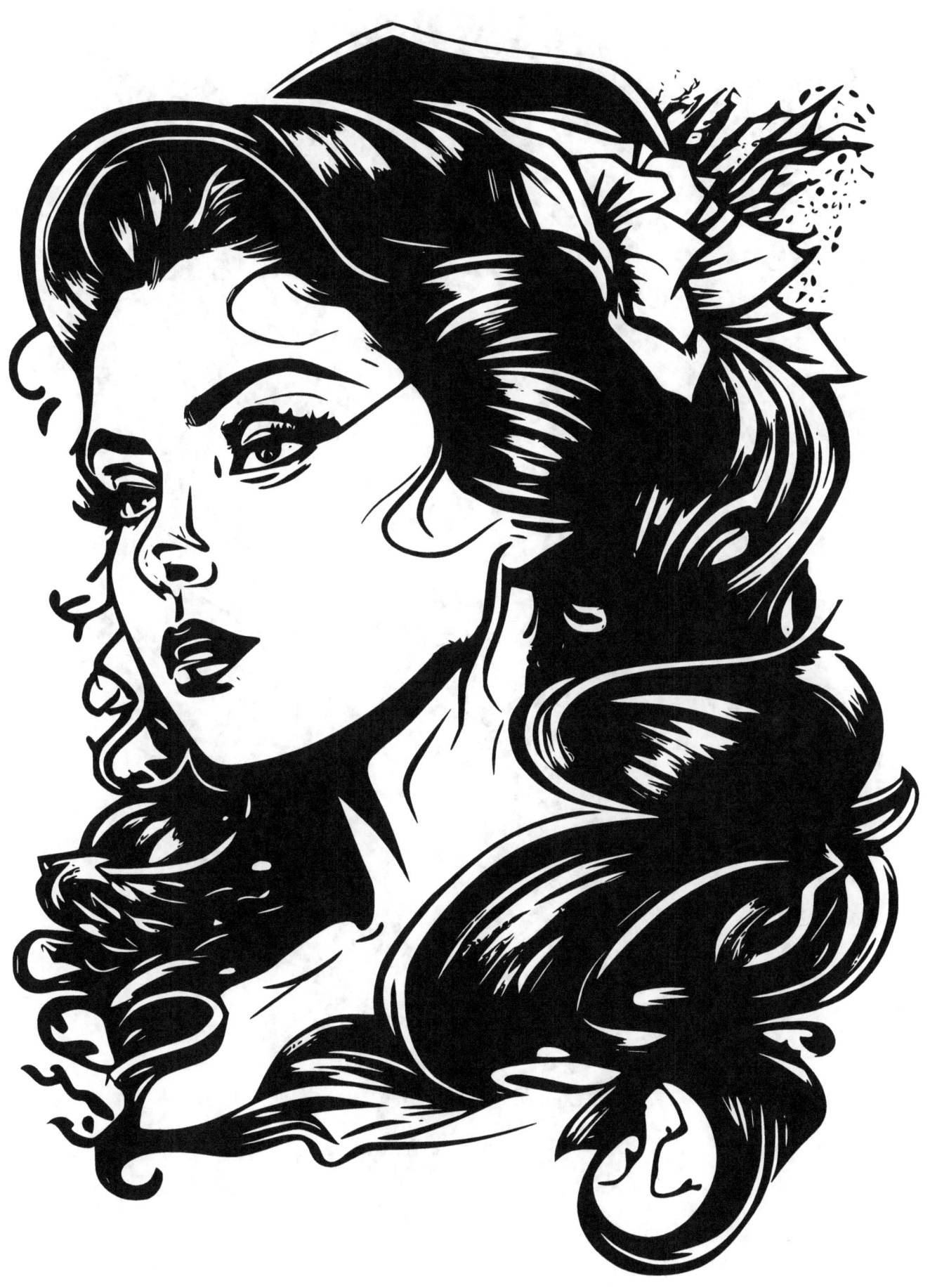

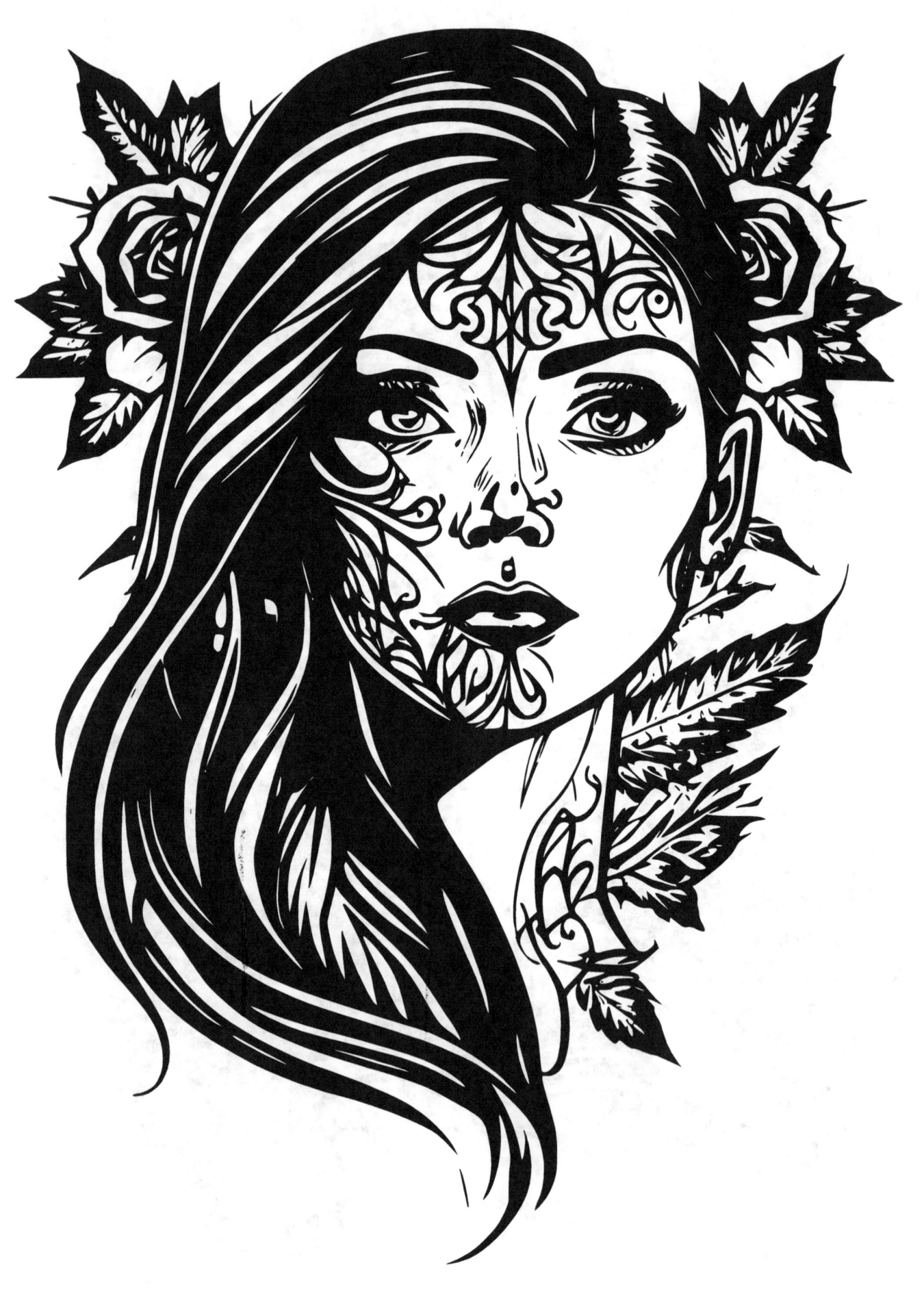

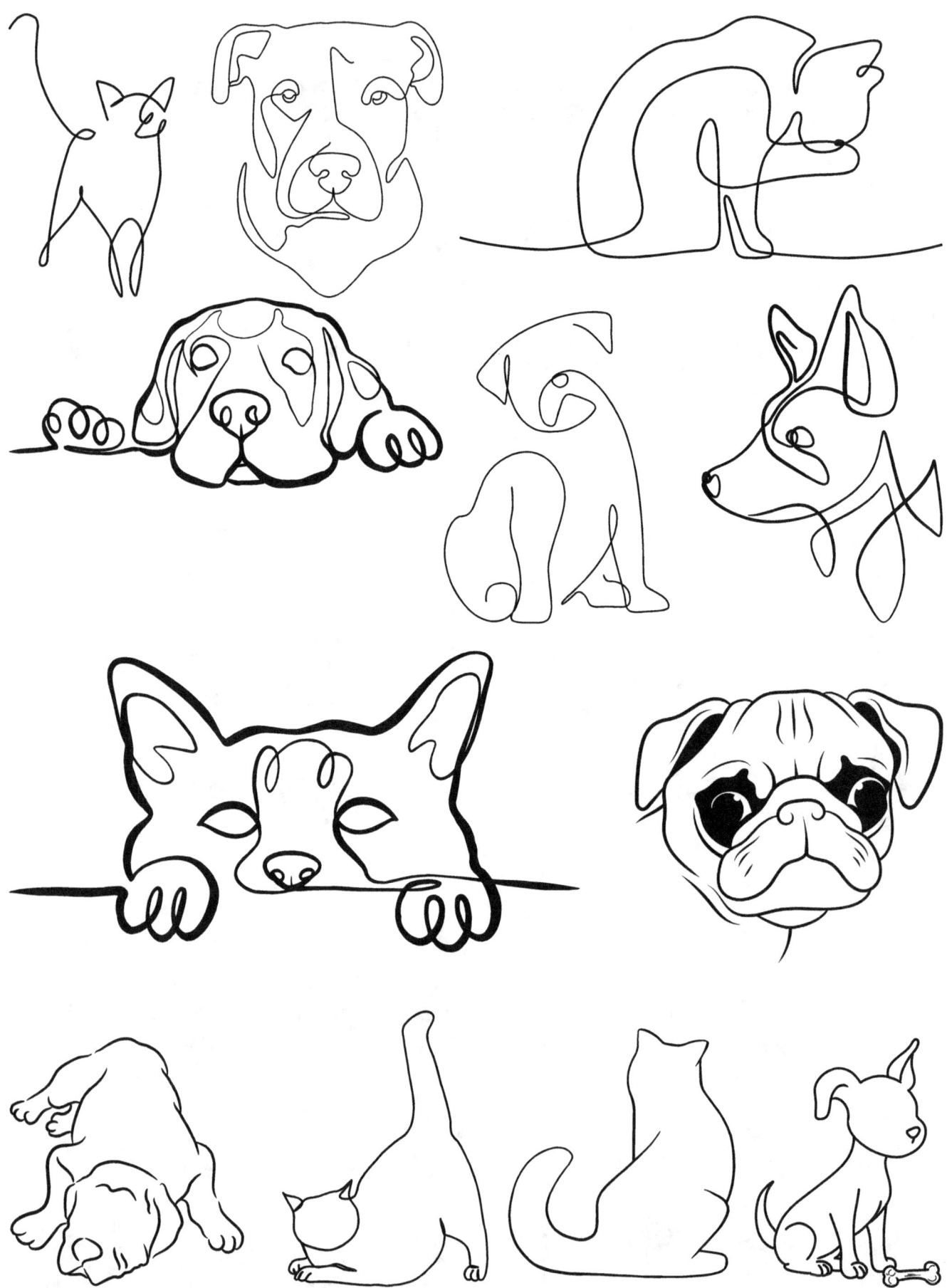

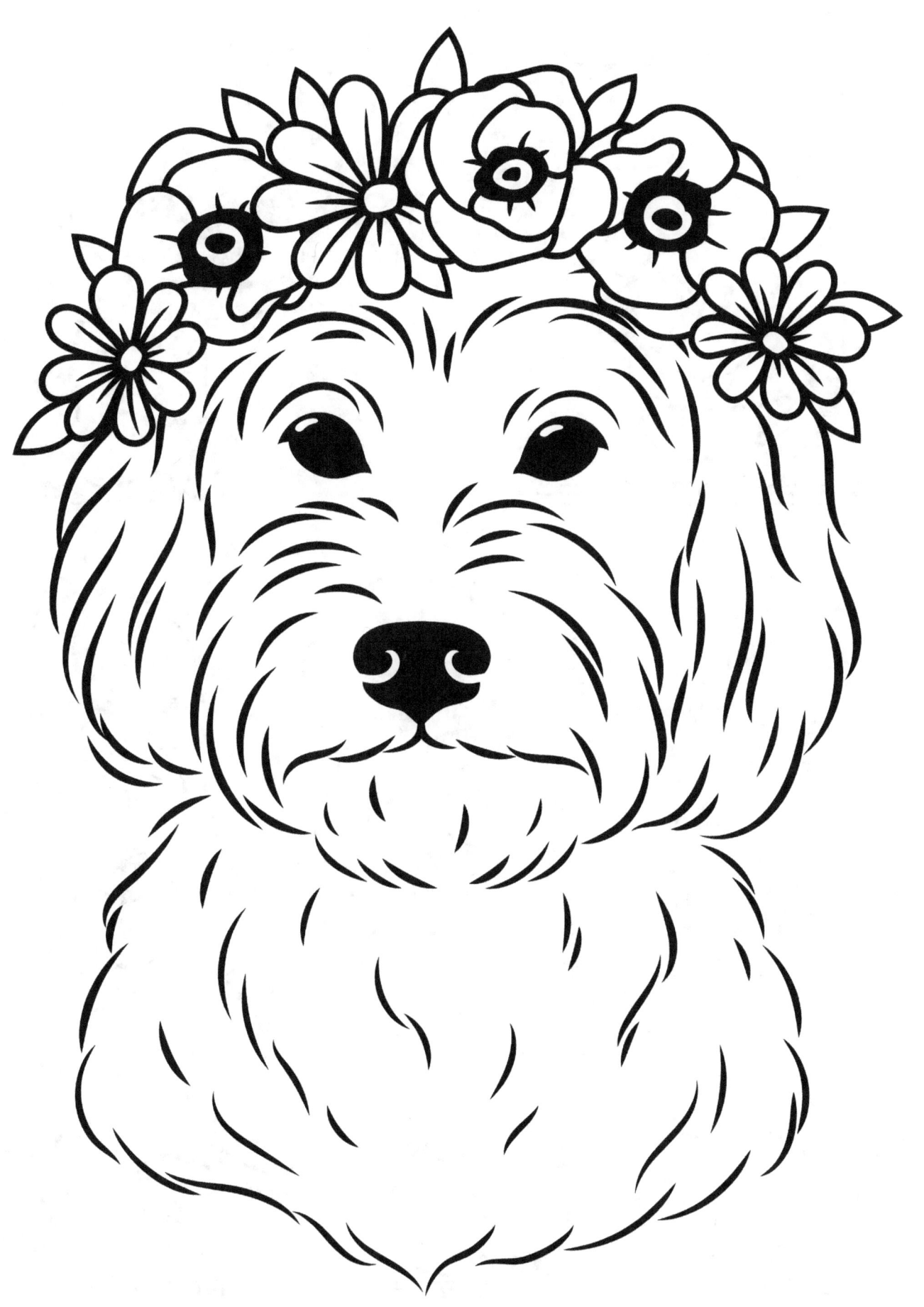

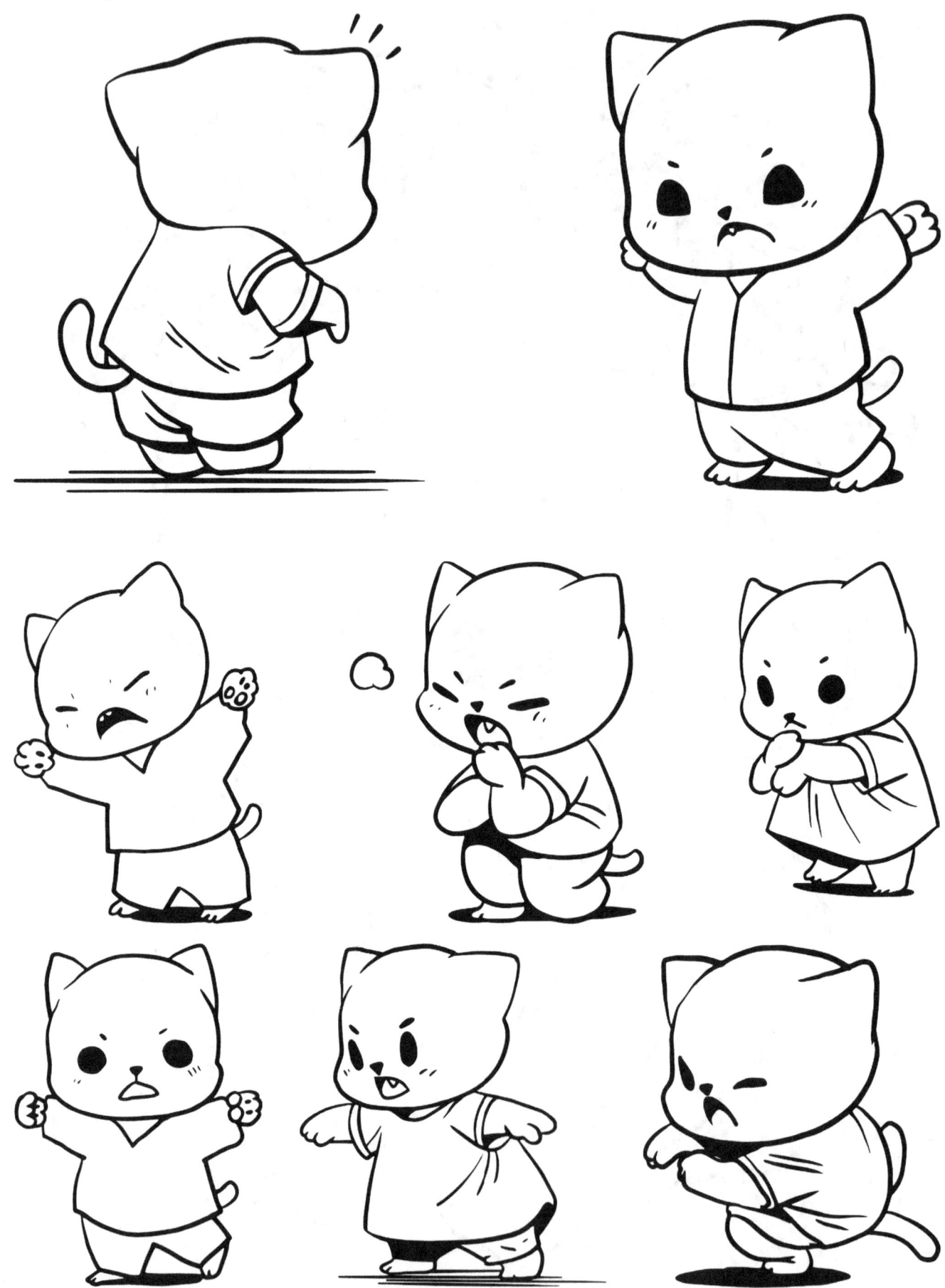

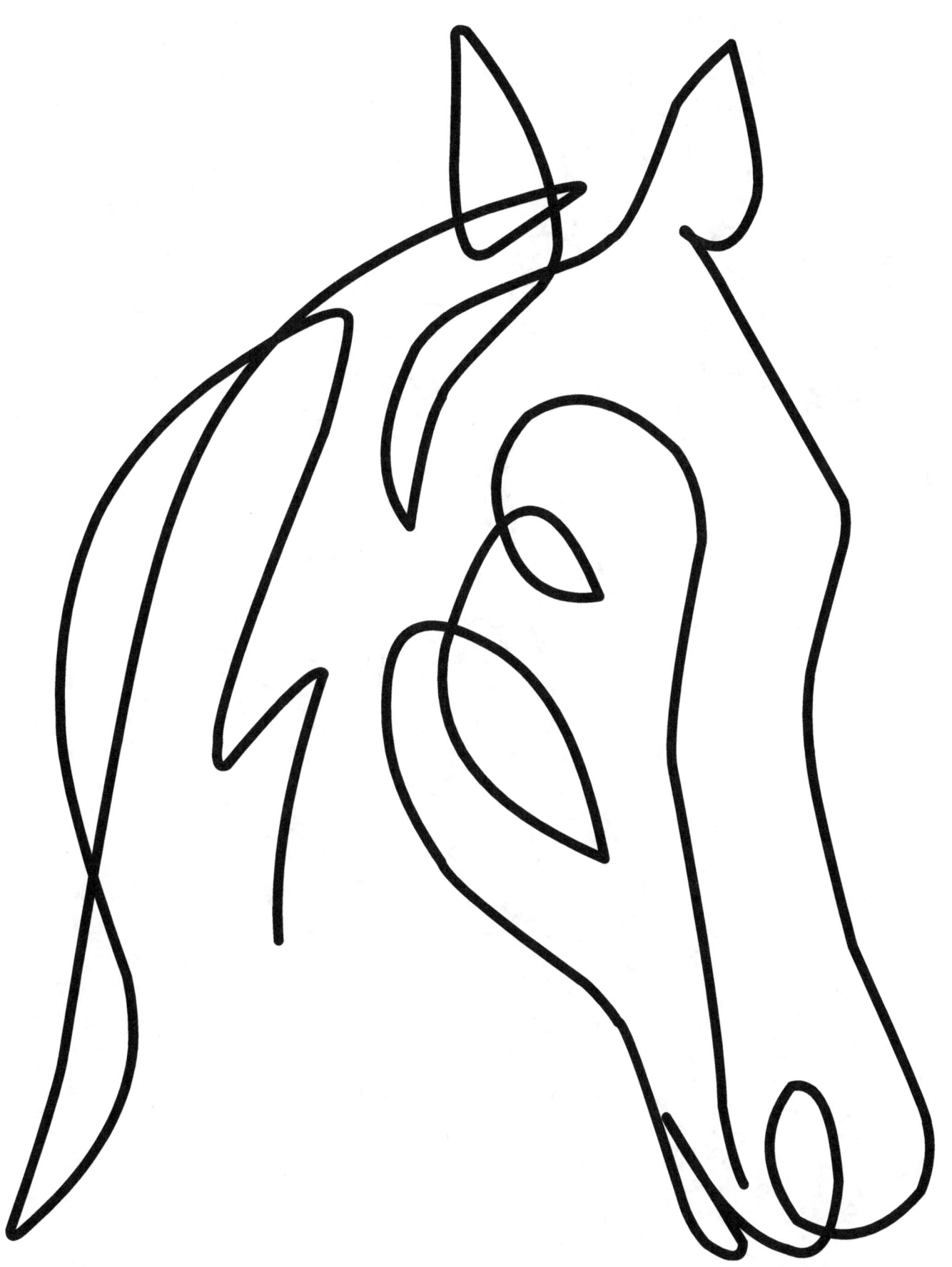

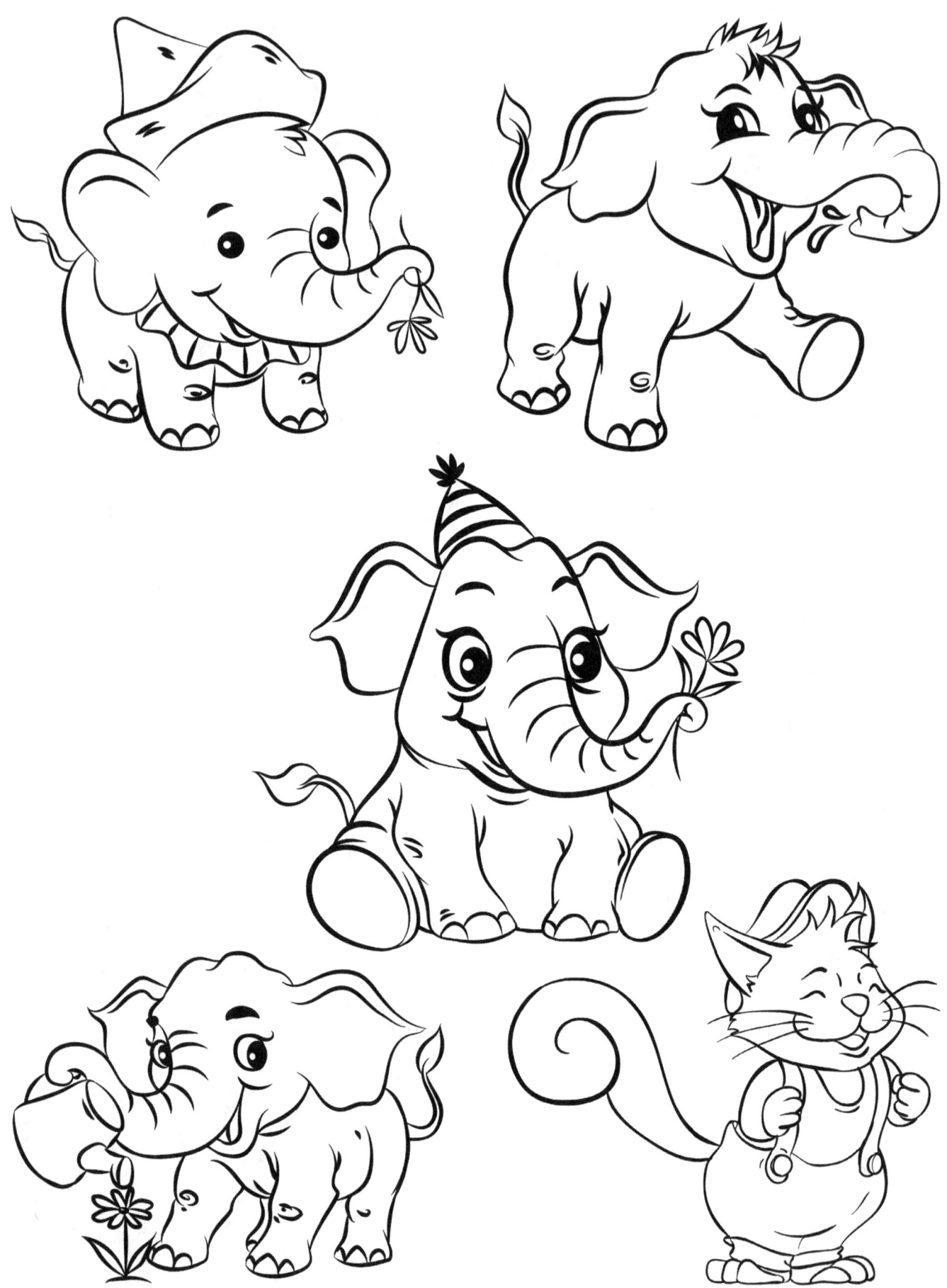

Thank you very much for purchasing one of my books! I'm glad to know that you enjoyed my work and I hope you found what you were looking for in it.

If you are happy with your purchase, I would love for you to share your opinion through a review. Your comments are very valuable to me and help me to continually improve.

Get a free small design book in pdf format.
To thank you for your support, I would like to invite you to scan the QR code where you can access the free download. I hope you enjoy this little gift and continue to enjoy my posts.
Thank you very much again for your purchase and your time! I will be happy to receive your comments.
Sincerely.